DOV[illegible]
DAYS

CW00919103

Compiled by
Whitehaven Hospital Research Group

The story of an ancient country house and estate which later became a hospital and eventually the headquarters of a world famous rallying organisation.

Dedicated to all former Dovenby residents and staff

First published in 2012 by Whitehaven Hospital WEA Research Group

©Copyright remains with Whitehaven Hospital WEA Research Group,
the individual contributors and originators of the images.

ISBN 978-0-9544112-4-4

Designed and printed by Firpress Ltd, 5a Buddle Road, Clay Flatts, Workington, Cumbria CA14 3YD

CONTENTS

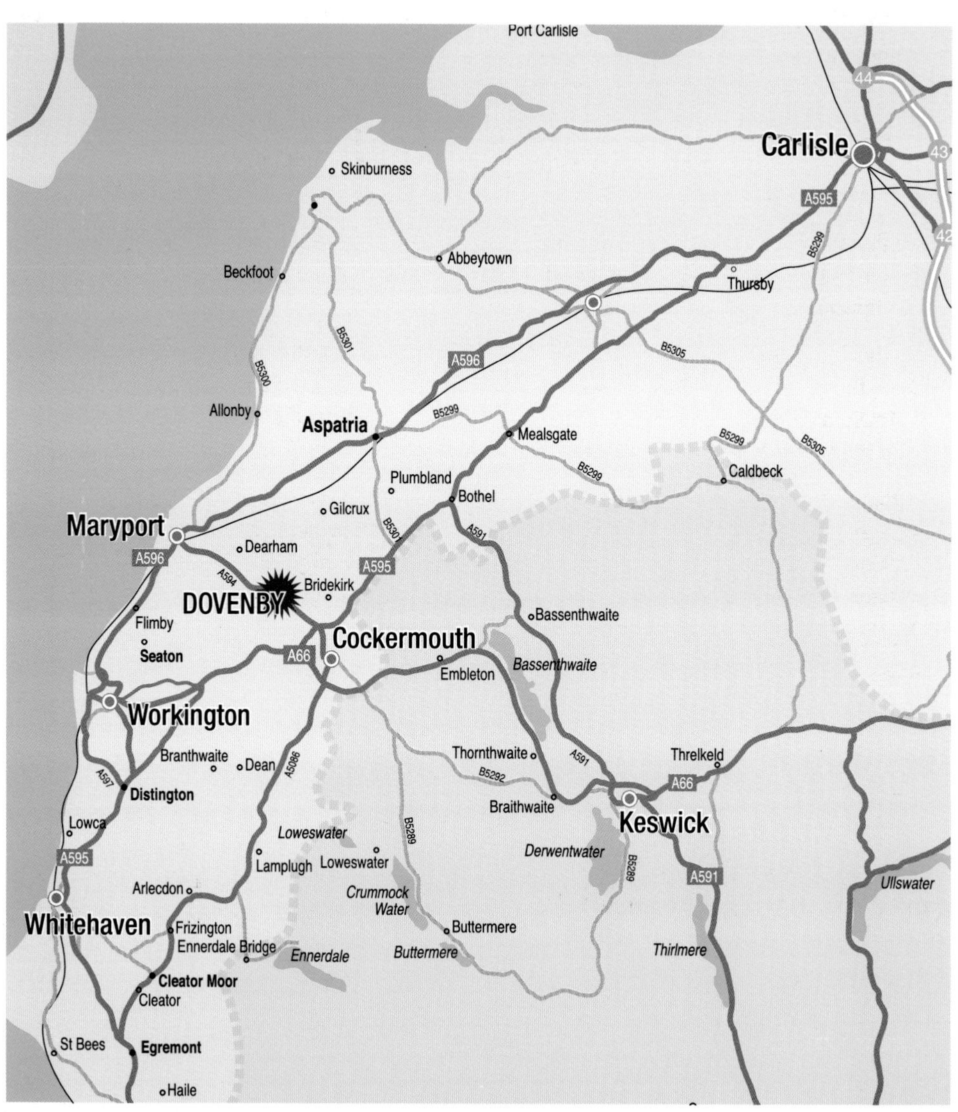
Port Carlisle
Carlisle
Skinburness
A595
Abbeytown
Beckfoot
Thursby
B5299
B5301
B5305
A596
B5300
Allonby
Aspatria
B5299
Mealsgate
B5299
B5305
Caldbeck
B5299
Plumbland
Bothel
Gilcrux
Maryport
A591
A596
Dearham
B5301
A594
A595
Bridekirk
DOVENBY
Bassenthwaite
Flimby
Cockermouth
Seaton
A66
Embleton
Bassenthwaite
Workington
Branthwaite
Dean
Thornthwaite
Threlkeld
A5086
A591
A597
B5292
A66
Distington
Braithwaite
Keswick
Lowca
Loweswater
B5289
A595
Lamplugh
Loweswater
Derwentwater
B5289
A591
Ullswater
Arlecdon
Crummock Water
Whitehaven
Frizington
Buttermere
Ennerdale Bridge
Ennerdale
Buttermere
Thirlmere
Cleator Moor
Cleator
St Bees
Egremont
Haile

INTRODUCTION

An enquiry by Workington library assistant, Lorraine Harper, as to whether a history of Dovenby Hall Hospital had ever been published, prompted the members of the Whitehaven Hospital Research Group to find out more. We were fortunate to co-opt Joan Warwick and Edyth Stephenson into our group, both of whom had worked at Dovenby for many years.

We were encouraged to proceed with our investigations by Alison Carswell, Senior Support Worker and the service users at Westlea Centre, Cockermouth, some of whom had been residents at Dovenby Hall.

Dovenby Hall Hospital was a residential establishment for people with learning disabilities between 1931 and 1996. The site was then taken over by Malcolm Wilson's M-Sport Ltd., a world famous rallying organisation.

With the kind permission of Malcolm Wilson and in particular Malcolm's mother, Pearl Wilson, the research group members and some former residents were invited to visit Dovenby. The house and grounds have been carefully restored much to the delight of those who had known the old establishment.

A coffee morning was arranged in May 2010. More than 70 people attended. They included former residents, nurses, a dentist, a physiotherapist, teachers, administrative staff and volunteers – in fact representatives of the whole Dovenby family arrived! We were overwhelmed by their enthusiasm and we were left in no doubt that we needed to record the many memories of Dovenby Hall.

Maureen Fisher
Whitehaven Hospital Research Group

Sketch of Dovenby Hall by Liz Percival

Research Group members visit Dovenby and meet Malcolm Wilson

*Researchers in the oak panelled room 2011.
L to R:- Maureen Fisher, Margaret Nelson, Pearl Wilson, Joan Warwick and Linda Davey.*

First coffee morning for former Dovenby residents and staff in May 2010

Former residents visit Dovenby

Charles and David certainly appreciated seeing the restoration of their former home.

Dorothy was most impressed by the rally cars!

CHAPTER 1

A BRIEF HISTORY OF DOVENBY HALL

The Dovenby Hall Estate, which comprised a large house and 115 acres of parks and woodland, was once the most important residence in Dovenby village, which lies 2.5 miles north-west of Cockermouth.

Dolfinby, later to become Dovenby, was the seat of Dolphin or Dolfin, son of Alward. The land was given to him in the 12th century by Waltheof or Waldeof, First Lord of Allerdale. The family held Dovenby from 1154 – 1189 and from 1216 – 1272.

The Hall began life as a pele tower, with stone allegedly taken from the Roman road which ran west of Dovenby Hall from Papcastle to Maryport. Pele towers were fortified keeps built along the border between England and Scotland to enable the owner to defend his goods and property from his enemies. An Act of Parliament in 1455 required each tower to have an iron basket on its summit so that a smoke or fire signal could give warning of an impending attack.

Families took refuge in the upper two storeys and livestock were gathered into the lower part during a raid.

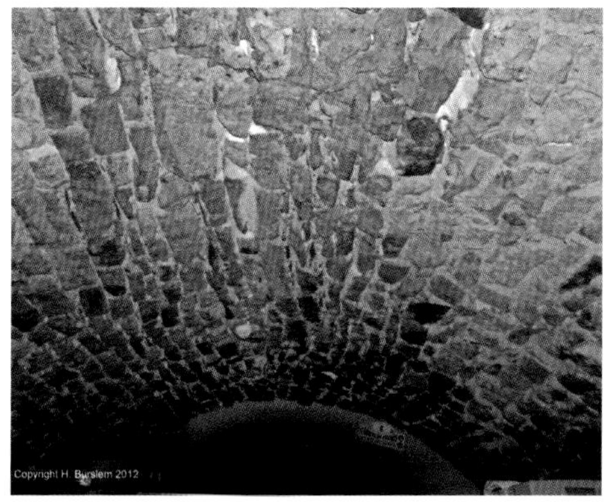

Tunnel-vaulted roof of ground floor chamber of tower

Dovenby Hall with pele tower

Openings or arrow slits allowed the tower to be defended. One opening or window remains facing the present staircase at Dovenby possibly providing ventilation for the ground floor. It is actually on an inside wall, because the hall we know today and the additional buildings were built around the tower in the 16th and 17th centuries. In some places in the tower the thickness of the walls is 49 inches!

Opening (now glazed) from the staircase. Photo Harold Burslem

Opening seen from inside the tower illustrating thickness of walls. Photo Harold Burslem

Dovenby Hall and tower circa 1930. Photo courtesy Hugh Ballantine Dykes

Dovenby Hall and tower today

Paddle steps to tower.
Photo Linda Davey

Beams at the top of the building – exposed only after renovations for M-Sport Ltd.

There is an unusual staircase leading to the roof of the tower. The ten steps which are known as paddle steps are very steep, designed for putting one foot on only.

The arched carriage entrance next to the tower leading to the rear courtyard may have been erected in the 16th century by the Lamplugh family who came to Dovenby in about 1400.

The rear extension which housed staff quarters and living rooms for the family was built by Richard Lamplugh of Ribton, possibly in the 17th century. One room was later panelled in oak by a member of the Dykes family who occupied the hall from 1791 to 1930.

Tower and archway

Building to right of the archway possibly once used as a private chapel – later became the boiler house.

THE GROUNDS

THE MULBERRY TREE

The mulberry tree in the grounds has its own history. It was grown from a cutting taken by a member of the Dykes family from an ancient mulberry tree which grew at their family home at Warthole or Wardhall before they settled at Dovenby in the late 18th century. It is said that Thomas Dykes, a devoted Royalist, hid in the tree at Wardhall when Cromwell's men came for him. His family brought him food every day. He eventually fell into the hands of Cromwell and was imprisoned in Cockermouth Castle where he died. It is from him and his refusal to follow Cromwell that the Dykes family take their family motto:

"Prius frangitur quam flectitur"

"You may sooner break me than bend me"

The rear extension 1997 and below in 2009

The Mulberry Tree. Photo Maureen Fisher

THE MEMORIAL

In a wood on the estate called Lake Walk, beside Bride's Beck there is a stone monument fenced off by railings. It is dedicated to the memory of Anne Francis Gunson who died of Tuberculosis in a special hospital in Edinburgh in 1837 aged 15. She was the youngest of three daughters of J. Gunson Esq. of Ingwell. When her eldest sister was courting Frechville Dykes of Dovenby Hall (whom she married in 1844) it is believed that Anne accompanied her on visits to Dovenby and took great pleasure walking in the woods despite her poor health. The monument was removed from Ingwell to Dovenby in 1860.

Photo courtesy M-Sport Ltd.

THE FAMILIES OF DOVENBY HALL[1]

(1154-1189) – (1216-1272)	Dolfin
(1216 – 1272) – 1305	Roger de Rolle
1305 – 1350	Thomas Lucy
1350 – 1398	Richard Kirkbride
1398 – onwards	Nicholas Lamplugh
	Lamplugh family
1577 – 1632	Sir Thomas Lamplugh
1632 – 1665	Dame Agnes Lamplugh
1665 – 1680	Molyne family
1680 – 1704	Richard and Mary Lamplugh
1704 – 1736	Mrs Mary Goodman (formerly Lamplugh)
1736 – 1763	Robert Lamplugh
1763 – 1764	Richard Lamplugh
1764 – 1768	Elizabeth Falconer
1768 – 1775	Mrs Elizabeth Irton
1775 – 1783	Reverend Thomas Lamplugh of Copgrove
1783 – 1791	Peter Brougham Lamplugh
1791 – 1930	Ballantine Dykes family

1 *CWAAS New Series Volume lxiv pages 256-263 "Some Portraits at Dovenby Hall" by A.R. Jabez Smith (Read at Rydal Church July 12th 1963)*

THE BALLANTINE DYKES FAMILY

The last family to make their home at Dovenby Hall, before it became an institution for the care of people with learning disabilities, were the Ballantine Dykes. They came to Dovenby in the late 18th century from their estate at Warthole or Wardhall, near Gilcrux, after Mary Dykes, the heiress of Wardhall, inherited Dovenby from her uncle, Peter Brougham Lamplugh. The Lamplugh family had owned Dovenby since the 14th century.

Mary married her cousin Joseph Ballantine Dykes in 1800. They had 11 children – 6 sons and 5 daughters. Joseph was High Sheriff for Cumberland in 1806.

Their eldest son, Frechville Lawson Ballantine Dykes, was M.P. for Cockermouth from 1832 -1836. He was also High Sheriff in 1842. He was decorated in the Crimean War.

His second son, Lamplugh Frechville Ballantine Dykes, inherited Dovenby and was followed in succession by his son, Frechville Hubert Ballantine Dykes, who was the last member of the family to inherit the hall. He and his family left in 1930 when the hall was sold, and moved to Broughton-in-Furness.

He had a great interest in model trains and had a model railway laid out in the generating house on the estate. Perhaps his enthusiasm stemmed from the fact that Dovenby Estate had its own private railway station. It was on the Bullgill to Brigham branch of the Maryport and Carlisle Railway Company, usually referred to as "The Derwent Branch" which opened to passengers in 1867. Frechville Lawson Ballantine Dykes had been chairman of the Company in the 1840s. It is very likely that the Ballantine Dykes family contributed most, if not all, the cost of the building of the station and the employment of the staff to maintain it. Apart from their personal use and the use of visitors and staff, supplies for the hall and houses on the estate were transported by train and also coal from the nearby Alice Pit.

Any passenger wanting to get off the train at Dovenby would have to inform the guard of their intention so that he could notify the engineman to make a special stop and a member of the station staff would operate a semaphore signal to alert the driver of anyone wanting to join a train at Dovenby.

Dovenby Station. Newspaper cutting.Source untraceable

During the General Strike of 1926, Colonel Frechville Hubert Ballantine Dykes drove the engines which must have caused some ill feeling among the miners but was probably a great thrill for him as a railway enthusiast!

The line closed in 1935.

Dovenby Station House today. By kind permission of the owner. Photo Dave Powell

Bridekirk Church
Photos courtesy of 'Visit Cumbria'

Many of the memorial plaques on the walls of Bridekirk church are dedicated to the memory of members of the Ballantine Dykes family. Photos Peter Davey

NANCY BALLANTINE DYKES

Interviewed on 12th May 2012 aged 92

Nancy was born at Dovenby Hall in 1919. She was one of three children; she had two brothers, one older, Thomas, and one younger, Joseph. Sadly, Major Thomas Lamplugh Ballantine Dykes of the Scots Guards was killed in North Africa during WWII aged 29. Joseph became a civil engineer with a passion for railways, kindled at a very early age at Dovenby.

Nancy was christened at Bridekirk church by Canon Sutton (more of him later) and well remembers walking to church from early childhood on Sunday mornings. She recalls a red door in the estate wall through which they got out onto the road. She understood that her mother had had the trees planted on the road to the church to shade them from the sun while walking!

Nancy had a series of governesses and nannies. One in particular made Nancy's life hell! She seemed to pick on her; always finding fault and making her feel totally inadequate. Nancy suffered from terrible "night terrors". She would wake up screaming and the nanny's treatment of these attacks was to get Nancy out of bed and make her stand on the cold linoleum in her bare feet in front of an open window.

Nancy writing letters at Dovenby aged about 10.
Photo Col. Hubert Ballantine Dykes

Thankfully she left and was followed by a Princess Christian College trained nanny, Nanny Quayle, who became a good friend to Nancy. This poor, young, newly qualified girl had to make her way to Dovenby by train. She had been told to make sure she told the engine driver to stop at Dovenby, where the chauffeur, who had been Nancy's father's batman during WWI, collected her and drove her up to the big house. By this time it was dark and the poor soul must have wondered what she was coming to. Life wasn't easy for a nanny in a large household as they were treated by the family as "a cut above" the other servants, who could be quite nasty at times. There was a butler, a cook, a head housemaid as well as other live-in and daily staff.

Nancy's mother Winnifred.
Photo Col. Hubert Ballantine Dykes

The nursery was on the first floor and was always warm as a fire was kept on all the time to dry and air clothes. It was when Nancy was much older that her nanny told her that she (Nancy) had woken up one night and said that she had seen a lady in a grey dress walk through the wall. Just one of the many Dovenby ghostly sightings!*

Nancy loved going up to the top floor of the house where the guest bedrooms were. In the dressing rooms there were lots of pictures and portraits. She used to like to make up stories about them. Sometimes the children from Dovenby School would come up to the house and they would take part in concerts and plays.

Nancy's mother had been an accomplished water colour artist in her youth but gave it up when she married Hubert and "got saddled with Dovenby" – Nancy's words! The pair met on a skiing trip to Switzerland and were married in 1911 at Lindale Church close to the bride's home, Merlewood, Grange in Cartmel. The wedding ceremony was performed by Canon Sutton of Bridekirk, who had not only christened the bridegroom but had also married the bridegroom's father and mother!

**There have been a number of reported "ghost" stories over the years involving doors which open and close without any apparent human intervention, swirls of mist appearing in corridors, footsteps heard but on investigation no-one could be seen, female figures appearing and disappearing and some have even described the sound of horse's hooves galloping close by – but not a horse in sight!*

Canon Sutton was quite elderly and very deaf when Nancy knew him. His daughter drove a Morgan car and had a very loud voice – it was the only way she could converse with her father - but she forgot that everyone else had normal hearing.

Col. Hubert Ballantine Dykes with Nancy and Joseph. Photo Col. Ballantine Dykes circa 1930

Nancy's father, Colonel Frechville Hubert Ballantine Dykes, like many of his ancestors, had a very distinguished career. He was educated at Christ Church, Oxford. He served as a Captain in the 2nd Battalion Scots Guards in WW1 and was mentioned in despatches three times. He was an excellent shot, having taken part in many shooting parties on the estate and so when he was posted to France his main task was to organise weapon training for the soldiers. He subsequently commanded 5th Battalion Border Regiment T.A. 1925-28. He was High Sheriff in 1923-24 and Lord Lieutenant of Cumberland from 1944-1949, following in the footsteps of many of his ancestors who had held these offices on numerous occasions.

Both parents were county magistrates. Nancy recalls that they were very busy people and were away quite a lot. She was sent to boarding school at Haywards Heath when she was aged about 13–14 years old.

Nancy became a very talented artist, working mainly in oils, and was a member of the United Society of Artists. One of her paintings "The Fishermen's Quarter, Ibiza" belongs to the National Trust and is now in Greenway, which was once the home of Agatha Christie in Devon. One of her last commissions was to paint a portrait of Father Gregory Freeman the Abbott of Douai Abbey.

Father Gregory Freeman by Nancy Ballantine Dykes Photo by Father Oliver Holt Douai Abbey

Dovenby Hall Photo Col. Ballantine Dykes

Nancy now aged 93

THE BALLANTINE DYKES AND CRICKET

Lamplugh Frechville Ballantine Dykes was the secretary of the first Cumberland County Cricket Club which was formed in 1884. This was the beginning of what was to be the family's long association with the game. The Ballantine Dykes had their own cricket pitch at Dovenby Hall where many local teams played their matches. During the time the Hall was used as a hospital, players continued to use the pitch and pavilion. Indeed for many it was their first introduction to Dovenby Hospital and people with learning disabilities as can be seen from stories later in this section.

The Dovenby Chairman's XI. Back Row L to R:- Tim Cowan, Steven Huddart, Paul Cusack, Lee Green, Richard Taylor, Daniel Chicken and Craig Moore. Front Row L to R:- Andrew Cowan, David Robinson, Tom Little, Michael Thompson and Andrew Denwood

Cricket at Dovenby

A Historic Occasion

At the suggestion of Club President,**Hugh Ballantine Dykes**,a match was arranged.at the end of last season.between the President's XI and the Chairman's XI to mark Dovenby's historic links with the family who first introduced cricket here over a hundred years ago.

The clubhouse was given a comprehensive 'autumn clean' and arrangements were complete in the food and wine department.but when the great day arrived the weather could not have been much worse.Nevertheless.both teams agreed that the occasion would not pass without some cricket being played.Eventually 23 overs were completed before the match had to be abandoned as conditions became increasingly treacherous.

Despite this.everyone agreed that the day had been a tremendous success.Our special guests.**Captain and Mrs.,Joseph Ballantine Dykes**,were delighted to see their sons and grandsons playing on the very field where their ancestors first played cricket in 1885.

A splendid buffet was enjoyed.during which.players and guests became better acquainted.It is hoped that we may be able to stage another of these games in the coming season.when the weather may be kind enough to allow us to have a barbecue for all to enjoy.

The players and officials who took part in this inaugaral and historic match were as follows:-

President's XI: Hugh Ballantine Dykes.Thomas Ballantine Dykes.Major Iain Dalzel-Job. Duncan Dalzel-Job.Alasdair Dalzel-Job.Malcolm Dalzel-Job.Keith Fisher. Richard Raymond.Andrew Mitchell.The Hon.Jamie Keith.Simon Fontes.

Chairman's XI: Tom Little.Michael Thompson.David Robinson.Richard Taylor. Daniel Chicken.,Andrew Cowan.Tim Cowan.Paul Cusack.Lee Green. Andrew Denwood.Craig Moore.

Umpires: Geoff Collyer and Derek Waite.

Scorer: Steven Huddart.

An extract from the Dovenby Park Chronicle edited by Tom Little 1991.

Front Row: Malcolm Dalzel-Job, Thomas Ballantine Dykes, Joseph Ballantine Dykes, Tom Little, Hugh Ballantine Dykes, Keith Fisher and Alasdair Dalzel-Job.

A SCARY CRICKET MATCH AT DOVENBY

John Ronaldson

I began my career with Cleator Moor Cricket Club in the early 1950s as a 14 year old. Our team comprised a few veterans, and a group of youngsters. We had a good blend, and we were always handily placed in the Cumberland League without setting any records alight. All local teams lived on a shoe string in those days, so Saturday journeys were made by all manner of transport ranging from bicycles and buses to decrepit old vans with very dodgy brakes and, if we were lucky, the occasional car.

We visited some diverse places including Millers Shoe Factory at Cockermouth, High Duty Alloys at Distington, 14 MU Depot, Metal Box Factory and Denton Holme at Carlisle. We played on some diabolical pitches but the team I particularly dreaded visiting was the notorious 'Dovenby Hall'. It all stemmed from my first visit. The humour of the experienced guys inevitably led to frequent 'wind ups' of the junior members of the team. Naturally, being the youngest I became an easy target. I'd heard about Dovenby Hall being akin to Garlands, supposedly a Mental Hospital housing many violent inmates. A Cleator Moor local chap, being a male nurse there, would also tell us tales, no doubt embroidered somewhat. I definitely did not want to play against such people. As the fixture came closer, the stories became more vivid until I was quite apprehensive at the prospect. I seriously thought of crying off. However, that being a coward's way out, I decided to accept my fate. As our bus travelled through Cockermouth the tension mounted. It was impossible to see over the high walls as we entered the impressive Dovenby Hall gates on that fine, hot and sunny afternoon. We parked directly in front of the impressive main building. As I saw the fine old structure with everything seemingly quiet and peaceful my fears were quickly allayed. As I made my way to the boot of the bus to help with the kit, I was aware of a couple of white coated staff entering the building. They were totally unconcerned at the prospect and I relaxed visibly. All those stories were fictitious and nothing but lies. There were obviously no dangerous inmates.

With my own bag over my shoulder and one hand on the team kitbag we set off to the ground which I learnt was round the corner and a couple of hundred yards away to into the area east of the buildings. We rounded the corner and progressed along the north side of the hospital. In the distance a group of a dozen or so men casually sauntered along the gravelled pathway. Absolutely nothing to worry about here I thought. Further along a few of the building's side windows were open and a soft wailing gradually emitted from within. The sound of unseen women's voices slowly increased as we walked on and a slight worry returned. Suddenly the distant characters saw us, and stopped dead in their tracks. After staring for a few seconds, they let out loud excited cries, followed by leaps in the air and a wild stampede towards us. This created a cacophony of various indescribable noises to come from inside the building. My worry disappeared to be replaced by sheer abject terror!!!! I dropped the kitbag, did a swift about turn and was off down the road like an Olympic sprinter. My colleagues were in stitches because having been there many times, they were used to the inmates antics in welcoming visitors and helping to carry equipment. When I was persuaded to return, albeit with more than a little concern, I was reluctant to release my bag to one of these "would be" helpers. When I finally gave in, he turned and sprinted away. I thought that was the last I would see of my boots, flannels etc. I was assured it would be safely deposited in the pavilion and so it proved along with all our other gear.

As we approached the ground, we saw a series of swings, slides, roundabouts and play equipment in a play area south of the pitch. Men were swinging to and fro, some in danger of doing complete circles as their friends egged them on with hoots and yells of encouragement and derision. After that introduction, I still felt it was incredible that these people were able to play a game of cricket seriously. It was only then that my team mates informed me that we were in actual fact playing the local village team who leased the ground from the hospital. What a rotten lot my team mates were!

I don't remember much about that first game as I was continually in a state of shock. I do recall that the inmates were the most enthusiastic group I had ever played in front of – cheering loudly the downfall of each wicket or big hit. While fielding and chasing one such massive hit, I was beaten by an inmate tearing in from the boundary. I arrived fractionally after him, rather flustered but most appreciative when he stopped the ball and quietly handed it to me. With a yell and a huge grin he returned to the boundary thoroughly happy to the delight of his mates.

The local team was lead by Dr Ferguson, a leading doctor at the Hospital. He wasn't a particularly good cricketer but a wily old fox, renowned for bending the rules without actually breaking them. Cleator Club members remember him without much affection due to some devious circumstances in an important match a couple of years later.

Both teams had progressed to the finals of the Burton Cup, the main trophy for Cumberland Senior League Teams. In those days teams tossed a coin to decide the venue for the final - no such thing as neutral ground. Dovenby Hall won the toss and the match was played at Dovenby on a Sunday following their home match the previous day. Saturday's pitch showed much wear and damage with no remedial repairs having been undertaken, the foot marks being filled in with rough earth and gravel. Adjacent to this was a well manicured pitch ready for action, obviously today's pitch. Our captain Donald Campbell strode out with Dr Ferguson, inspected this new strip and tossed up for the choice of who batted first. Dr Ferguson won the toss and asked Cleator to bat. But when our opening batsman left the pavilion they were amazed to see the wickets had been placed on the old damaged wicket!!

A Cleator complaint followed but the status quo remained as Dr Ferguson refused to submit. Play eventually started and our batsmen were obviously - to say the least – ill at ease. Stevenson, their fiery hostile fast bowler, with a mane of jet black hair, ran in and banged the ball down onto the wicket. Each ball was unpredictable as one would shoot along the ground while the next whistled past the batsmen's eyes. No crash helmets in those days! Cleator was in disarray and soon skittled out for a paltry 21 runs. Unbelievable!! The match was over in less than two hours and that included the excellent tea break served in the pavilion with the help of inmates – the only thing Cleator enjoyed that day! A special meeting of the League committee later ruled that all cup finals were to be played on neutral grounds. Oddly enough both teams played out the next year's final at Whitehaven and thankfully Cleator gained ample revenge with an easy win – but not by such a prolific margin.

I never looked forward to the Dovenby Hall fixtures, and always felt uneasy.

MORE DOVENBY CRICKETING MEMORIES

Gilbert Johnstone

I joined Dovenby Cricket Club in 1958 and spent a thoroughly enjoyable time until the club folded in 1969. Dr Ferguson was the Dovenby representative on the team.

During my time at Dovenby I met some lovely characters who lived in the hospital. Firstly Isaac, who actually made one appearance for the cricket club v Wigton. He was a keen supporter and used to attend our local derby v Cockermouth at Sandair. The day was made jollier for him as he was allowed two bottles of beer! Next Frank, a reserved person for whom I took an apple to each home match. He would not take it directly from me so I put it on top of a fence post from where he eventually took it. During the afternoon he would, at some point, slowly walk alongside me and thank me for the apple. David, another hospital resident was forever requesting that I bring him some knitting needles. In the interests of safety I always made the excuse that I had forgotten them. This seemed to satisfy him until the next match.

Mid week friendly cricket was played at the hospital, which on a dreary evening gave an eerie feel to the ground. This was sometimes an advantage as some of the visiting players seemed a bit frightened!

I remember three visitors from Denton Holme Cricket Club who always attended matches to support their club. There was Billy Sinclair, his wife and her sister. Whilst Billy smoked his pipe the sisters were busy knitting. Billy told me on numerous occasions how much the three of them enjoyed their Saturday afternoons and evenings at Dovenby, especially if it coincided with one of the outdoor concerts given by local organisations.

It was a lovely setting in which to play cricket with everything done by the hospital staff from preparing the ground to providing the teas. My twelve years visiting Dovenby Hospital grounds were very, very enjoyable and a part of my life I am happy to reflect upon.

CHAPTER 2

BEFORE DOVENBY HALL HOSPITAL

There have been many attempts to bring about change in order to improve the lives of people with a learning disability. Their lifestyle today is vastly superior to that of their predecessors.

In literature we have only to look at the life of "the village idiot" as he was referred to in Flora Thompson's book, "Larkrise to Candleford". Here was a young man probably born profoundly deaf, who could not speak or communicate and therefore had no education. The strange sounds that he made in an effort to speak only resulted in fear and ridicule from the adults and children around him who called him "Luney Joe". After the death of his mother, who had always staunchly defended him, he was sent to the County Asylum.

Also the poor crippled character, Michael, played so well by John Mills in the film "Ryan's Daughter", illustrates the attitudes of the community towards those with any kind of infirmity – mental or physical.

Even William Wordsworth, whose poems often reflect the life and characters he observed around him, describes in his poem "The Idiot Boy", how Johnny, the boy in the title, having been sent by his mother, Betty, to fetch the doctor for a sick friend, spends the whole night riding round the countryside listening to the owls hooting and admiring the moon. When his mother eventually finds him, having frantically searched the countryside when neither he nor the doctor had appeared by midnight, he is quite unperturbed – unlike his mother and the neighbour who, by the way, made a dramatic recovery!

The final verse describes how much he enjoyed the unaccustomed freedom to do as he pleased even if he did get a little mixed up with his recollection of events.

"And thus to Betty's question, he,
Made answer, like a traveller bold,
(His very words I give to you,)
'The cocks did crow to-whoo, to-whoo,
And the sun did shine so cold.'
--Thus answered Johnny in his glory,
And that was all his travel's story."

William Wordsworth "The Idiot Boy"

Interestingly, these examples also show that, in the past, people with disabilities often remained in their communities being cared for by family members or reliant on "The Parish" until the 19th century when government legislation introduced registration, classification and detention. How remarkable then, that today, the emphasis is on "Care in the Community".

What follows is a brief history of the legislation which influenced the treatment of people with learning disabilities from very early times to the beginning of the 20th century.

Although the list may appear rather long and laborious it was felt necessary to include this information as it illustrates the labels used to describe those with learning disabilities which were in common usage throughout the centuries but which would not be tolerated today.

1400s	Lunatics admitted to hospitals. Treatment consisted of chaining and whipping.
1500s	It was recommended that the insane should be "kept in a closed chamber and should have a keeper whom he fears". Witchcraft was linked to madness (which included people with learning disabilities at that time).
1700s	Earlier laws against witchcraft were abolished
1744	**Rogues, Vagabonds and other Idle and Disorderly Persons Act.** This Act made the distinction between lunatics and vagrants/paupers.
1774	**Regulation of Madhouses Act**
1794	**Feeblemindedness** (a term used to describe those with learning disabilities) was considered to be transmitted through the generations. The feebleminded were considered to be a group reproducing at a greater rate than the general population. Treatment at this time included bleeding and emetics.
1828	**Lunatic Asylum Regulation Act**
1834	**Poor Law Amendment Act** This separated people considered unable to contribute to the economy into workhouses.
1886	**The Idiots Act** This was the first time that the needs of the mentally handicapped were specifically addressed by legislation. In addition to workhouses people with learning disabilities were often admitted to lunatic asylums and prisons. The Act introduced registration, inspection and admission to specialised asylums.
1890	**The Lunacy Act** This Act did not discriminate between the mentally ill and the ***mentally retarded.***
1909	**A Royal Commission** was set up to investigate "the problem" of the feeble minded.
1913	**The Mental Deficiency Bill** People with learning difficulties now identified as distinct from the mentally ill.
1913	**The Mental Deficiency Act** This legalised the detention of individuals with varying degrees of ***mental defect.*** The Act established four classes of ***mental deficiency:*** **1. Idiot** – unable to guard themselves against common physical dangers, such as fire, water or traffic. **2. Imbecile** – could guard against physical dangers but were incapable of managing themselves or their affairs.

3. Feebleminded – needed care or control for protection of self or others.

4. Moral Defectives – In particular this influential Act made it possible to institutionalise women with illegitimate children who were receiving Poor Relief.

1927 The Mental Deficiency Act
This gave Local Authorities statutory responsibility for providing occupation and training. Mental Deficiency was defined as "a condition of arrested or incomplete development of the mind, existing before the age of 18 years, whether arising from inherent causes or induced by disease or injury".

1929 The Wood Committee
WWI (1914-1918) delayed the implementation of the recommendations of the 1913 Mental Deficiency Act but the findings of the Wood Report resulted in the acceleration of the policy which recommended that 100,000 individuals suffering from Mental Deficiency be immediately institutionalised and advocated that the formation of self sufficient colonies would cater for all groups of mental defect regardless of age or level of disability. The term colony was eventually replaced with the term hospital with the implementation of The National Health Service Act (1948) under which the control of the colonies was transferred from local councils to Regional Hospital Boards.

1948 National Health Service Act
Treatment becomes free at the point of access.

1950 European Convention on Human Rights

1957 Royal Commission on Mental Deficiency and the Law relating to Mental Illness
This paved the way for the new Mental Health Act.

1959 Mental Health Act

1. **Repealed all previous Acts.**
2. **Made provision for the care and treatment of mentally disordered persons and the management of their property and affairs.**
3. **It placed emphasis on:**

a. Informal admission
Admisson to hospital to be known as "Informal Admission". As much treatment as possible both in and out of hospital should be of a voluntary nature.

b. Compulsory admission
Only those people ill enough to require care and treatment for their own sake or for the sake of their families and the community, or who are unwilling to go to hospital would be subject to compulsion.

Where possible, treatment and training will be available in the community.

4. **The term Mental Defective is abolished and redefined as:**

a) Subnormal
b) Severely subnormal
c) Psychopathic personality

1969	**The Howe Report** Report of the Committee of Enquiry into allegations of ill treatment of patients and other irregularities at the Ely Hospital, Cardiff.
1971	**White Paper** Better services for the Mentally Handicapped. It advocated a 50% reduction in hospital places by 1991 and an increase in the provision of local authority based residential and day care. It also called for an end to custodial methods of care in hospitals and recommended re-training of hospital staff.
1972	**Wolfensberg –the concept of normalisation.**
1979	**Jay Report** Report of the Committee of Enquiry into Mental Handicap Nursing and Care. It re-emphasised the need for local authority-led care and a service philosophy based on the Principles of Normalisation.
1981	**Principles of Normalisation** In the UK, the Principles of Normalisation adopted were those interpreted by O'Brien and Tyne as the Five Service Accomplishments. These have become the developmental goals which organisations, then and now, strive towards: ***Community Presence*** – ensuring that service users are present in the community by supporting their actual presence in the same neighbourhoods, schools, workplaces, shops, recreational facilities and churches as ordinary citizens. ***Choice*** – ensuring that service users are supported in making choices about their lives by encouraging people to understand their situation, the options they face and to act in their own interest both in small everyday matters and in such important issues such as who to live with and what type of work to do. ***Competence*** – developing the competence of service users by developing skills and attributes that are functional and meaningful in natural community, environments and relationships, i.e. skills and attributes which significantly decrease a person's dependency or develop personal characteristics that other people value. ***Respect*** – enhancing the respect afforded to service users by developing and maintaining a positive reputation for people who use the service by ensuring that the choice of activities, locations, forms of dress and use of language promote perception of people with disabilities as developing citizens. ***Community Participation*** – ensuring that the service users participate in the life of the community by supporting people's natural relationships with their families, neighbours and co-workers and, when necessary, widening each individual's network of personal relationships to include an increasing number of people.
1989	**White Paper – Caring for People** Confirmed the Government's commitment to the development of locally based health and social care services.

1990 NHS and Community Care Act

To provide the necessary support structures to enable (when possible) people to remain in their own homes, thereby reducing demand for long term care.

Other Key Factors in bringing about change for people with Learning Disabilities:

National

- British Institute for Mental Health. National Development Team
- National Association for Mental Health
- MENCAP
- Joint Finance Provision – Joint Care Planning Teams
- Development of Advocacy and Self Advocacy groups

Local

- Dovenby closure and Community Development
- Aldingham Hall Project
- Lyndhurst – Pre-discharge facility
- Community Mental Handicap Team
- Development of Community Mental Health Nursing Association
- Joint Working Partnerships

THE OPENING OF DOVENBY HALL COLONY

On October 1st 1931 Dovenby Hall Colony was declared open by Canon Sutton of Bridekirk, Chairman of Cumberland County Council, in the presence of a large gathering of County Councillors from Cumberland and Westmorland, members of Carlisle City Council and others interested in mental welfare work.

The attendees first gathered in the recreation room which was initially provided in one of the outbuildings adjacent to the hall itself. Colonel Dudgeon presided and in his address he praised the Cumberland, Westmorland and Carlisle Joint Committee for the Mentally Defective for bringing about this step forward in the progress of looking after the care of the health, of not only the two counties and the Borough of Carlisle, but of the nation.

He observed that this was not the time to talk of the condition known as Mental Deficiency which so affected the vitality of the nation but to feel grateful that through the coordination of the three bodies that Dovenby Hall Colony had been opened. He noted that previously cases had been scattered about in various institutions but that now they could all be taken to Dovenby and all conditions graded. He went on to say that when they were graded the inmates could receive perfect care, nursing, protection, treatment and training. There would also be education for the children. He forecast that when the buildings were completed there would be 800 to 1,000 people in the Colony. He also gave assurance that there had been no waste or extravagance in the construction and layout of the site insisting that the design of the buildings was for efficiency and not for show.

He then introduced Cannon Sutton, describing his years of work for the county, his leadership of the governing body and his connection with Bridekirk parish over the past fifty years, before inviting him to declare Dovenby Hall open.

Canon Sutton began by expressing his gratitude for the honour of opening the building. He had known the mansion for fifty years and could recall the time in 1881 when he was there to welcome Mr Lamplugh Dykes (sic) and his bride when they came from India and the great rejoicing later that year when their son and heir was born. He had always been assured of a welcome and accommodation at the house in the winter when his wife had to go to the south of France. He noted that the architect, Mr Morton, had made very little alteration to the house. He recollected that the recreation room in which they were meeting was once the stable block and when he was younger and enjoyed riding he had only to send down to Dovenby Hall and a hunter would be provided for him.

He reassured the public, especially those living nearby, that Dovenby was not an offshoot of Garlands, the large mental hospital in Carlisle, but that it was a place where girls and children could learn flower and raffia work. For the women there would be laundry work, housework, needlework, cookery, basket, rug and brush making and the use of a stocking machine.

The boys and men would learn carpentry, tailoring, wood chopping, gardening and agricultural work which would prove to everyone that the Colony was an educational establishment and nothing whatever to do with Garlands. He was sure the Matron and staff, backed by the Committee, would take great care of those entrusted to them and the delightful surroundings would help the poor people who came to the Colony.

He then proceeded to knock on the front door with a small ivory mallet and declared the Colony open. He remarked that he had never known the front door to be locked and this was the first time he had ever had to knock and ask permission to go in!

Canon Sutton was thanked by Mr Pattinson who pointed out that the Joint Committee owed a great deal to him for his guidance in the purchase of Dovenby Hall. A previous plan suggested by the Board of Control to upgrade and expand Prudhoe Hall at a cost of £180,000 was overthrown because it was felt very strongly that the mental defectives at present residing in this part of the country should not be taken away to the north east, where it would be very difficult for parents and relatives to visit them and also the cost was unaffordable. Dovenby had been adapted in a most pleasing way for under £40,000.

The Mayor of Carlisle seconded the vote of thanks and added that Dovenby was a real home from home which would enable the inmates to do the best they could for themselves regarding education and health.

The buildings were then inspected by those present and afterwards tea was served.

One of the invitees, Lady Mabel Howard, made a plea for people to send toys and books for the children and also vases for flowers to decorate the rooms would be greatly appreciated.

L to R: - T B Harston (Clerk of Joint Committee), Colonel J H Dudgeon (Chairman of Joint Committee), Mr G H Pattinson (Chairman of Building Committee), Miss Bevan (Matron), Lady Mabel Howard (Chairman of House Committee), Canon Sutton of Bridekirk who performed the opening ceremony, Mr Morton, (Architect), Mr F W Tassell (Mayor of Carlisle), Mr C W Allan-Hodgson (Chairman of Finance Committee) and Mrs Dent from Westmorland.

CHAPTER 3

DEVELOPMENT OF THE SITE AND SERVICES

Following the recommendations of the Wood Committee (1929) which stated that individuals suffering from mental deficiency should be housed in colonies, where they could be provided with a safe environment, be properly graded, receive nursing care, taught useful occupations and be "educated", the Cumberland, Westmorland and Carlisle Joint Committee for Mental Defectives began to look about for a suitable site. There may have been a number of locations available but, perhaps persuaded by Canon Sutton who had known the estate for many years, Dovenby was purchased in 1930. It is believed that the initial cost was in the region of £40,000 and adaptations to outbuildings amounted to a further £28,000.

Shepherd House

Storey House today

A few days after the opening ceremony the first "inmates", as they were labelled, were transferred from Milnthorpe Institution to Dovenby Industrial Home or Colony as it was then known. The first 65 females were housed in the mansion house itself.

Shortly afterwards two double storey buildings opened. These were Pattinson House and Sutton House. Each of these accommodated 60 residents. This meant that 165 beds were immediately available but it became clear that the Colony would have to increase considerably in size. In the late 1930s three new units were opened. These were Hodgson House, Howard House and Storey House. These units provided places for another 150 residents. *(Note how the houses were named after members of the Management Committee, former Matrons and the former Medical Superintendent.)*

During the Second World War, under the Government's Emergency Scheme, Dovenby took in residents from Shotley Bridge Institution in Durham and Prudoe in Northumberland which filled it to capacity. After the National Health Service came into being in 1948 the name changed to Dovenby Hall Hospital and was administered by the local Health Authority.

In the 1950s Bevan and Harston Houses were built, followed by the Occupational Therapy Department in the 1960s. Accommodation for children was added in the mid 1960s. This consisted of McHugh Villa for the boys and Punnett for the girls. In the beginning school classrooms were in the courtyard in the building which had once been the coach house but after the building of Punnet and McHugh, Storey House became the school. It was used as a sanatorium at one time during an outbreak of Tuberculosis among the residents. Dobell and Johnston-Sharp Villas were added in the 1970s. The last villa to be built was Shepherd which opened in 1975 as a pre-discharge unit for 30 residents, who, it was hoped, could eventually live life in the community.

Dougie Dixon, who was the Site Engineer in the 1950s and 60s, recalls some of the staff accommodation round the perimeter of the site during that era.

Linden House .... Ian Collins – Finance Officer
Orchard House .... Male Staff quarters. Later became Nurse Training School
Dovenby Cottages .... Reg Dixon – Hospital Secretary

Not on the map:

North Lodge	Nicholas Rennac – Catering Manager
South Lodge	Dougie Dixon – Hospital Engineer
Station House	Bill Simpson – Group Engineer
Storey House	Children's Centre

Dougie also affirms that for many years while he was in post the site was self-sufficient with its own skilled tradesmen.

Ronnie Casson	Gardener
Dougie Dixon	Engineer
Bill Simpson	Group Engineer
Raymond McAvoy	Electrician
Bob Penrice	Plumber
Bill Scott	Joiner
Austin Walsh	Gardener
Bill Warwick	Master Builder – Mason

Photos of plaques by Holly Monkhouse

DOVENBY SITE (post 1975)

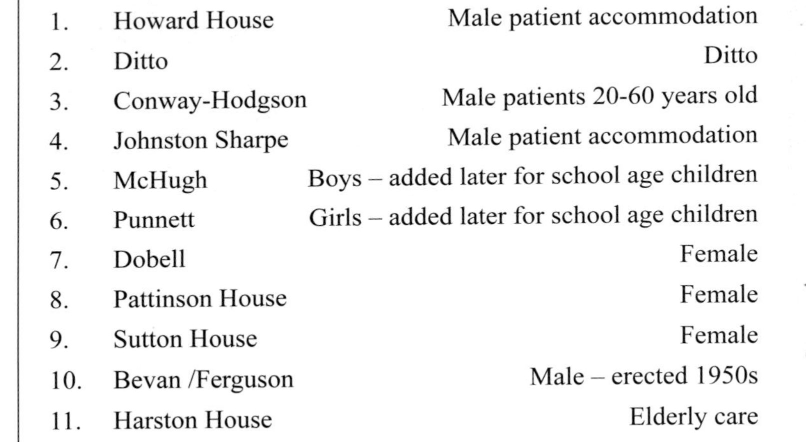

1.	Howard House	Male patient accommodation
2.	Ditto	Ditto
3.	Conway-Hodgson	Male patients 20-60 years old
4.	Johnston Sharpe	Male patient accommodation
5.	McHugh	Boys – added later for school age children
6.	Punnett	Girls – added later for school age children
7.	Dobell	Female
8.	Pattinson House	Female
9.	Sutton House	Female
10.	Bevan /Ferguson	Male – erected 1950s
11.	Harston House	Elderly care
12.	Shepherd Villa	Last to be completed in 1975
14.	Occupational Therapy and Further Education	
17.	Recreation Hall	
18.	Sports Pavilion and Tennis Courts	
22.	Dovenby Hall	Nurses' accommodation, Doctor's Office and Administration
29.	Gardener's workshop and store	
30.	Mortuary	
32.	Boiler House – pre 1930 the building housed a private chapel and laundry for Dovenby Hall	

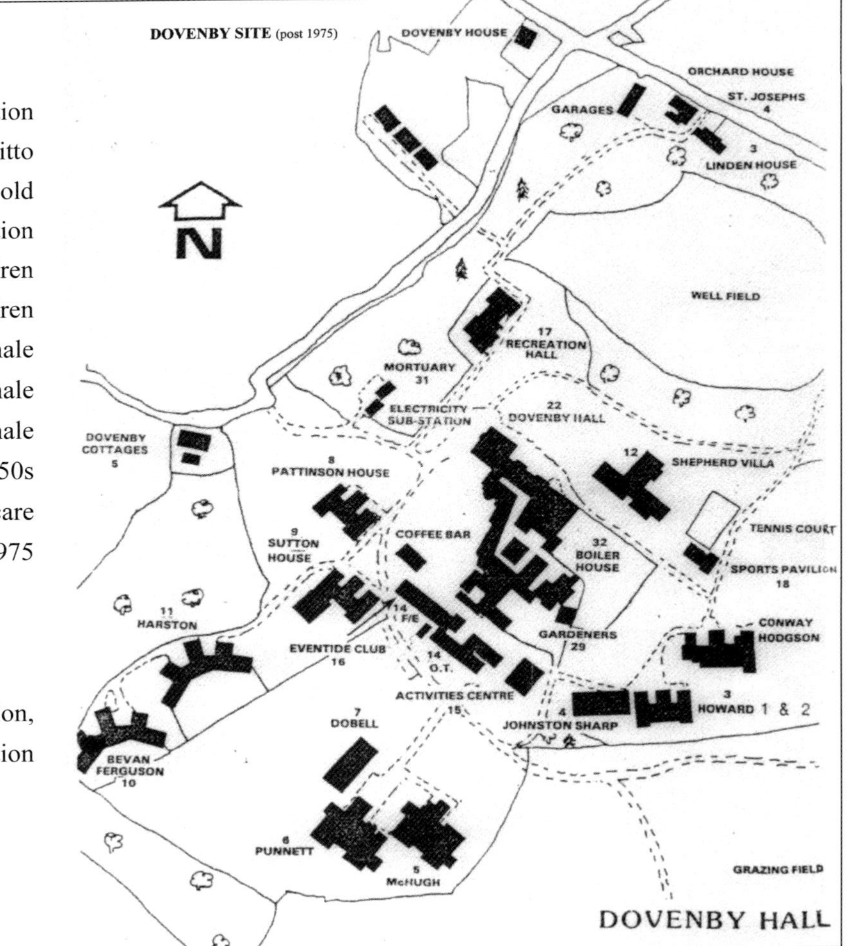

The power supply for the site was provided by large battery plants housed in the Generator/ Boiler room where a full- time boilerman was employed.

The lighting on the roads between the various buildings was not good in the early years which must have been pretty nerve wracking for staff having to move between wards or visit the mortuary during the night, until a new system was introduced.

There were also painters and decorators, general labourers, van drivers and tractor drivers.

A team of chefs and kitchen staff sent hot meals to the wards three times daily and provided catering for the staff.

Florence Clark recalls a large kitchen garden tended by a gardener and some residents. Also pigsties and one resident, Robert, kept hens beside the pavilion.

All the laundry was done on site.

A bespoke tailor, Mr Hutchinson, made suits for the male staff and male patients. He was a master craftsman who sewed while sitting crossed legged on a bench!

Seamstresses made dresses for the female patients. These were initially air force blue, maroon or bottle green and all the same design. Later, in the 1960s, dresses were made of Crimplene. They did sewing repairs, alterations, made curtains and soft furnishings.

Sewing Room ladies circa1955-61. Photo Judith Smith

Photograph contributed captioned "Sewing room Betty". Perhaps the lady on the right? Photo Belle Hadley

An in-house cobbler repaired shoes. As more funding came available shoes and clothing were purchased from local retailers. Mr Pattinson of Cockermouth supplied shoes. He was only one outlet of many used at the discretion of the ward manager from whom supplies were obtained. A resident hairdresser was on site and a barber visited regularly for the gent's haircuts.

The Recreation Hall was multi purpose. In the daytime it was an extension of the Occupational Therapy Service. The staff held functions there and each Sunday a Catholic church service was held at 4pm which was open to the general public.

All the wards, initially, had one domestic cleaner. In the early years some of the more able residents worked alongside the staff. A local man who was serving his time as a plumber remembers visiting the site with his employer to carry out a task alongside the Dovenby plumber. They were taken to the workshop and were most impressed by the quality of the welding work being undertaken by one of the residents. Another young visiting tradesman got a real telling off from the ward sister when he forgot to lock the door to the toilet to which he had been given a key, with strict instructions always to keep it locked. He realised his mistake when he saw a resident dancing down the corridor with a lavatory seat around his neck. Apparently this individual had a penchant for ripping off lavatory seats whenever the opportunity presented itself!

The Dovenby on site tradesmen were paid a small amount to take on a resident and train them in their particular skill. Similarly, some of the ward cleaning and laundry was carried out by residents, under supervision.

The Marchon factory at Whitehaven provided bottles and "tops" to be assembled. Textel Fibres sent cardboard rolls which had the fibres still attached to them. The residents removed the fibres, cleaned the rolls and returned them to the factory to be re-used. Some former residents recall the "stick house" where they chopped sticks and tied them into bundles to be sold by the local coal merchant. Those undertaking these jobs were paid a small fee on completion of the task. Both male and female residents appeared to gain a great deal of satisfaction from the range of activities which were offered. Far from feeling exploited, the opportunity to do a job of "work" was appreciated and enjoyed by many of those who took p rt.

In later years state benefits were paid to residents which they could spend as they chose. They were allowed to buy what they wanted and were encouraged to save towards days out and holidays. Participation in mundane tasks to earn pocket money with which to buy treats was no longer obligatory or necessary. They no longer had to wear hospital "uniform".

Medical and Nursing Services

Initially the site was presided over by a Medical Superintendent, a Matron and their Deputies.

Nursing care was provided by a mixture of untrained and trained staff. Some of them were the product of the hospital's own training school (see later chapter) which was established in 1959.

Dental Services

Mr. A.B Gibson, Consultant Dental Surgeon, held surgery sessions in the evenings. Mr Gibson and Consultant Anaesthetist Dr. H Corfield carried out the treatment. At this time there was no dental nurse available and so a ward nurse assisted. Sister Joan Warwick and Charge Nurse John Baker fulfilled this duty occasionally. The most common form of treatment was dental extraction. Following the reorganisation of the National Health Service in 1974 Cumbria Area Health Authority took over the dental services for the inpatients of Dovenby Hall Hospital. The West Cumberland Hospital Anaesthesia department covered the sessions on a rota basis with a consultant anaesthetist, theatre technician, dental nurse and a recovery nurse in attendance.

Ophthalmic Services

Heals opticians from Cockermouth carried out regular eye tests on the residents.

A young assistant to the optician recalls that it wasn't the easiest job in the world and she many times had to "rescue" a frightened customer from under the table!

The site had its own Pharmacy and Mortuary.

Aerial views of the site (post 1975) with names of buildings

1 Dovenby Hall
2 Pele Tower
3 Shepherd Villa
4 Cricket Pavilion
5 Hodgson House (E1 & E2)
6 Howard House (I & II)
7 Coffee Shop / Hairdressing Salon
8 McHugh Villa
9 Punnet Villa
10 Dobell
11 Occupational Therapy
12 Johnston Sharpe
13 Kitchens
14 Staff Dining Room
15 Swimming Pool (Therapy Pool)
16 Stores
17 Laundry
18 Sutton House
19 Pattinson House

"There were two things which could be seen from the moon, one was the Great Wall of China and the other was Dovenby night lights!"
Dougie Dixon

CHAPTER 4
THE EARLY YEARS

I couldn't stop at home any longer 'cos I needed a bit of help. Me dad says to me, "I don't know how you'll come on when I'm not here, Martha." I says, "Oh, I'll be all right." He says, "I don't think so."

After my dad died one of my sisters came to stay with me for a few weeks and she wanted me to go away. Then I went to another sister for three months and it was while I was there that word came for me to go into Dovenby. I got word one day and I had my clothes packed and was in Dovenby the next day.

This was how one resident describes her introduction to Dovenby. She had problems with mobility and had obviously been cared for at home until the death of her parents. She remained in Dovenby for more than thirty years until the 1990s when she moved into a group home in Cockermouth.

Martha remembers the attitude of some the public when they were taken on outings. "Look out here comes the Dovenby lot!" was one of the comments that upset her. When they were allowed to go into Cockermouth on their own, her friend used to suggest that they changed into their own clothes instead of the Dovenby "uniform" which consisted of a straight dress tied in the middle, but Martha argued that it didn't matter what you wore you had to get on the bus at the Dovenby stop so everyone knew where you were from! However she had very fond memories of Dovenby and the staff.

Her story is typical of many who came to Dovenby. Some were transferred from other institutions such as Shotley Bridge, Milnthorpe, Moss Side, Rampton and local Workhouses.

Others remember being sent to Dovenby as children as young as three or four.

Further reasons for admission were:

- Family unable to cope
- Family troubles
- In trouble with the police
- Unmarried mother

Some residents had no idea why they were there. One young woman said her mother "put her out." She went on to say that she was referring to her step-mother who didn't want her.

Another young woman had been sent to Dovenby because she struck her mother.

Fit young men were sent out to various farms to plough or harvest. Some worked in the Dovenby vegetable garden. Female residents helped out with ward cleaning, laundry and kitchen duties.

The patients were strictly segregated. Male patients lived on one side of the hospital looked after by mainly male staff. Female patients lived on the opposite side. They were always strictly chaperoned and would be escorted by a nurse, sometimes two when moving around the grounds. At dances, they were not allowed to dance with the same person more than twice. Any attempt at more was frowned upon.

The more able residents were allowed to leave the hospital for a few hours each Saturday to visit Maryport or Cockermouth; men only one weekend and women only on alternate weekends. Their names, departure time and return time were strictly recorded in the ward record book.

The residents were entertained regularly by concerts and pantomimes which were performed by the staff or visiting groups such as Women's Institutes and musical societies. The Recreation Hall had excellent facilities for these events.

Two sisters, Susan and Janie Graham, worked as nurses at Dovenby in the very early years. Susan left when she got married. Janie stayed on and married Patric Cahill, a male nurse. She became a ward sister.

(Information and photographs kindly contributed by Harry Doloughan)

Susan Graham

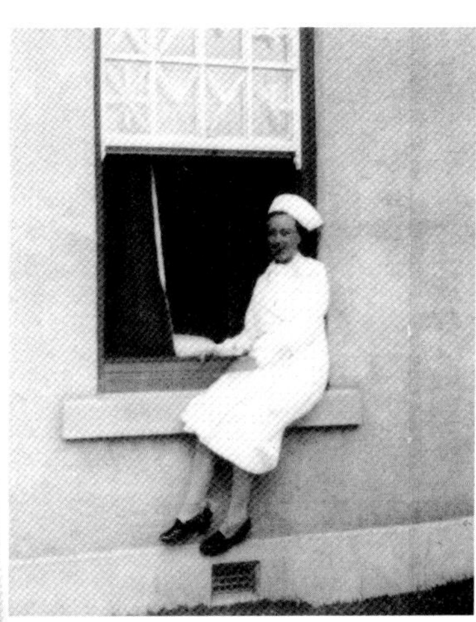

Susan Graham (probably 1939 – note tape on windows)

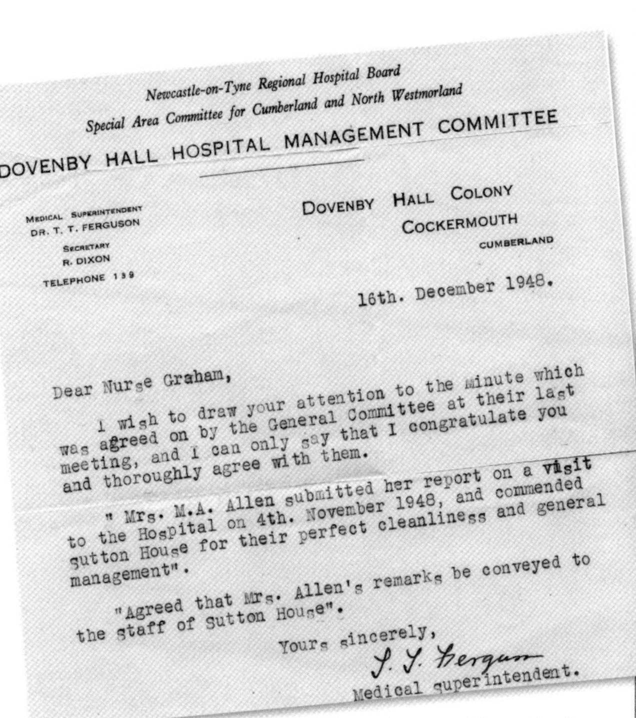

Newcastle-on-Tyne Regional Hospital Board
Special Area Committee for Cumberland and North Westmorland

DOVENBY HALL HOSPITAL MANAGEMENT COMMITTEE

MEDICAL SUPERINTENDENT
DR. T. T. FERGUSON
SECRETARY
R. DIXON
TELEPHONE 139

DOVENBY HALL COLONY
COCKERMOUTH
CUMBERLAND

16th. December 1948.

Dear Nurse Graham,

I wish to draw your attention to the minute which was agreed on by the General Committee at their last meeting, and I can only say that I congratulate you and thoroughly agree with them.

" Mrs. M.A. Allen submitted her report on a visit to the Hospital on 4th. November 1948, and commended Sutton House for their perfect cleanliness and general management".

"Agreed that Mrs. Allen's remarks be conveyed to the staff of Sutton House".

Yours sincerely,

T. T. Ferguson

Medical Superintendent.

Letter to Sister Graham from Dr Ferguson. Note the address.

Sister Janie Graham (later Cahill)

Janie and Patric Cahill

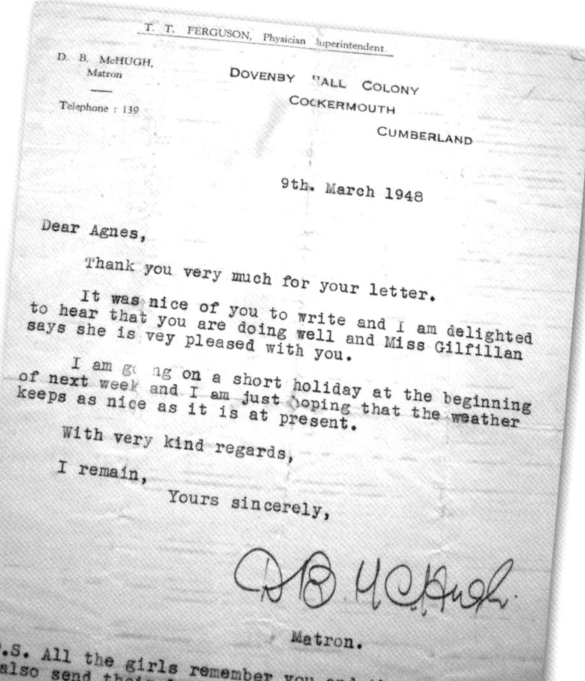

T. T. FERGUSON, Physician Superintendent.

D. B. McHUGH,
Matron

Telephone : 139

DOVENBY HALL COLONY
COCKERMOUTH
CUMBERLAND

9th. March 1948

Dear Agnes,

Thank you very much for your letter.

It was nice of you to write and I am delighted to hear that you are doing well and Miss Gilfillan says she is vey pleased with you.

I am going on a short holiday at the beginning of next week and I am just hoping that the weather keeps as nice as it is at present.

With very kind regards,

I remain,

Yours sincerely,

D B McHugh

Matron.

P.S. All the girls remember you and the Office Clerks also send their love.

Agnes(left) to whom the letter above refers was able to find employment outside the hospital.

Right: Nurses probably 1940s

Photos Belle Hadley

A typical ward dining room at Christmas. The door on the left lead to a small sitting room, while the one on the right housed outdoor coats and shoes

Dr. T. T. FERGUSON J.P., L.R.C.P. & S.E.D., L.R.F.P.S.Glas.

In 1947 Dr Thomas Traill Ferguson was appointed as the first physician superintendent of Dovenby Hall Hospital, a post he held for 25 years until his retirement in 1972.

Dr Ferguson trained in Glasgow and had held the post of deputy medical superintendent at Lennox Castle until he joined the RAMC in 1942. He was with the 1st British Corps at the "D" Day landings in Normandy and was twice mentioned in dispatches.

He returned to civilian life in 1946 and after a year as acting medical superintendent at Lennox Castle he was appointed as the first superintendent of Dovenby Hall Hospital where he instituted the "open" wards system and the short term care of patients which allowed carers to have some respite. He was proud of the hospital and its dedicated staff and he provided opportunities for education for nurses long before the official training school was established by giving lectures. These were discouraged by the Joint Committee!

AT

RED CROSS INSPECTION AT DOVENBY HALL

L to R:- Mrs T.T. Ferguson, Matron McHugh, Lady Graham, Sir Fergus Graham, (Lord Lieutenant of Cumberland), Sir Franklin Gimson K.C.M.G. and Dr. T.T. Ferguson. Photo courtesy Cumbrian Newspapers

Dr Ferguson became the first director of child guidance clinics in West Cumbria. He was interested in all forms of sport and played for various teams at rugby, cricket and tennis. He retired from Dovenby in 1972 but remained active in the local community. He was a district councillor and justice of the peace, retiring as Chairman of the Bench in 1977.

He was honorary Vice President of the Cumbria Branch of the British Red Cross Society who awarded him the Society's medal of honour. Red Cross rallies were often held at Dovenby.

COUNTY RED CROSS PARADE AT DOVENB

Newspaper coverage of Red Cross rallies - Courtesy Cumbrian Newspapers.
Red Cross inspection 1959. Photo courtesy Cumbrian Newspapers

Dr and Mrs Ferguson.

***1953** L to R:- Nurse Mary Percival, Sister Conway (Deputy Matron), Arthur Chandler, Sister Young, Not Known, Joyce Fletcher, Nina Ferguson, Matron McHugh, Dr Ferguson, Gladys Croft, David Gray, Mrs Ferguson, Not Known.*

***1950s** Front Row L to R: - Not Known, Lorna Kilbride, Dorothy Drummond, Joyce Fletcher, Ann Hodgson, Not Known, Gladys Hutchinson. Middle row L to R:- Sister Cahill, Sister Ida Hutchinson, Gwen Featherstone, Sister Johnson, Matron McHugh, Kath Walker, Rita Dixon, Not Known. Back Row L to R: - ? H Price, Not Known, Sister Young, Not Known, Gwen Nicholson, ?, Nurse Watson, E Thornthwaite. Photos Joyce Gray*

Charge Nurse Jack Franklin and an unknown nurse circa 1955-61. Photo Judith Smith

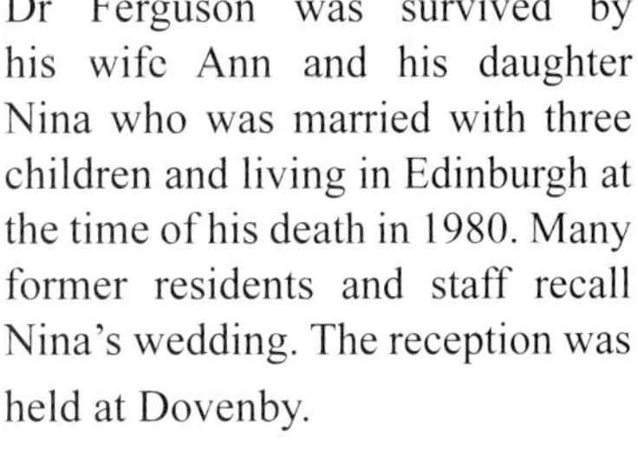

Dr Ferguson was survived by his wife Ann and his daughter Nina who was married with three children and living in Edinburgh at the time of his death in 1980. Many former residents and staff recall Nina's wedding. The reception was held at Dovenby.

L to R :- Joyce Fletcher, Joseph Nicholson and Gladys Renac in the 1950s. Photo Joyce Gray

Garden Parties were very popular. Photos Belle Hadley

A staff gathering in 1948 after a garden party. Photo supplied by Lilian Lister

Dovenby staff and their families regularly took part in pantomimes

Right: Gentleman 4th from right is Stanley Stevenson Deputy Charge Nurse McHugh Ward. Photo Belle Hadley

Aladdin 1962-63 Photo Liz Percival

THE EDUCATION AND TRAINING OF SCHOOL AGE CHILDREN AT DOVENBY HALL

In the beginning the school was overseen by the Management Committee. It was situated within the courtyard, having two classrooms, a kitchen and a stage. Education and training in the classrooms at Dovenby Hall Hospital tended to be in the form of the crafts, sewing, carpentry and domestic skills encouraging the children to acquire knowledge and experience appropriate to their intellectual ability.

As time evolved, the Local Education Authority was required to provide education for this group of children, recognised as being emotionally maladjusted with behavioural difficulties or disadvantaged by social handicap – as well as having learning disabilities. Some were from broken or inadequate homes resulting in being deprived of a normal home life.

Evacuees were transferred to Dovenby from the North East during the Second World War and several remained there.

There was a formal process in place to assess and recognise the degrees of intellectual retardation. The teaching staff were skilled in encouraging and helping the children to understand simple language and tasks encouraging reading where possible and communication using Makaton sign language.

In the late 1960s Storey House was refurbished and became the school, retaining the veranda. Additional classrooms, cloakrooms, gym, showers and bathroom facilities were built resulting in much improved conditions. By this time there were extra pupils and teaching staff. The number of pupils attending the school was 50, some of whom were residential and some were day pupils. Day pupils attending Dovenby School came from the surrounding districts of Aspatria, Silloth, Workington and Penrith. This was a time of enormous change at Dovenby School.

The residential pupils walked to school escorted by members of the nursing staff. If it was raining they were given transport to school. The boys who were residential were cared for by Deputy Charge Nurse Stephenson and Charge Joe Lowther. The girls were cared for by Sister Blaylock followed by Sister Hazel Dawson and Deputy Nursing Sister Jean Lothian. Soon school uniform was introduced, navy in colour with jackets, shirts and ties and smart shoes replacing previous uniform of ill-fitting garments and shoes.

On the lst April 1972 the responsibility was transferred from the Health Service to the Education Department. More improvement followed with the erection of school gates, climbing frames, balancing benches, and a staff room. Within a decade a vast improvement had taken place as a special care unit had been added. R.N.M.H. Student Nurses spent three months placement as part of their training schedule. Mary Wells-Walker was Head Teacher at Dovenby School; Mary Hayton was Deputy Head Teacher.

Mary Wells-Walker was an accomplished pianist, music being her specialist interest. She arranged school assemblies with music and actions, all enhanced by the delivery of a new piano. The Variety Club of Great Britain was approached for assistance to buy a new mini-bus. In 1973 £1,000 was raised towards the cost. At that time actor, Charlie Drake, was appearing in the London show the "Pyjama Game". Mary Wells-Walker and a member of her teaching staff, Chris Shaw, were invited to the show and presented with a new mini-bus. They drove out of London at dawn to return to Dovenby with their prize.

The school was then able to take the pupils on outings into the Lake District, Morecambe and on holiday to Torquay. Visits into Workington for shopping were organised for the older pupils. Summer fetes and garden parties were held with displays of the children's work. There was country dancing with new dresses for the ladies and new cummerbunds for the men. Pantomimes were organised in winter, special dance routines being taught. The casts' costumes were enhanced by paper flowers prepared by Sister Chandler.

Three ponies were kept at Dovenby looked after by Pat Tyson, who took the children riding on Thursdays. There was a pony trap built by Jim Stamper especially for the pupils, an exciting experience for the children. Riding for the Disabled became available at Bassenthwaite and then at The Calvert Trust.

Nationally, significant change was taking place with the 1976 Education Act and Government commissioned enquiries resulting in a new concept of "Special Educational Needs". The aim was to integrate some of these pupils into main stream schools. The Warnock Report of 1975 strengthened this concept. Pupils at Dovenby were becoming fewer in number and so closure took place in 1983 some being transferred to Mayfield School at Hensingham along with their teaching staff. The closure was celebrated by staff and pupils holding a huge bonfire and firework display.

Sister Hadley, Storey House. Photo Belle Hadley

Sister Lilian Lister and children, Storey House. Photo Lilian Lister

Members of Maryport Boys' Club hand over the rocking horse to Dovenby Hospital special school. Photo courtesy Cumbrian Newspapers

CHAPTER 5
NURSE TRAINING

The first matron of Dovenby Colony was Miss Jean Bevan. She and the nursing sisters were fully trained nurses. Other staff, such as Lillian Lister who lived locally, applied and were employed as "attendants". In 1939 labour was short (due to WWII) and anyone thought suitable was duly interviewed and given one month's trial. There were approximately 400 beds at this point in time. The attendants lived in the Nurses' House just outside the estate grounds. They wore white overalls with green braid on the collar and white caps. They had two days off per week when they walked or cycled home. Every three months the staff rotated to a different ward or went on night duty. Wages were brought from Carlisle and wage packets were handed out on the main staircase in the Hall, each nurse moving 'up one' as their turn came.

During WWII when Prudhoe Hospital was commandeered by the military, some residents were evacuated to Dovenby and never returned. Gas masks were issued to staff and patients and regular safety drills were carried out. The "blackout" was rigidly observed and Lilian remembers a delivery of navy wool coats, enough for all the staff to have one!

With the introduction of the National Health Service in 1948, training began for nurses to specialise in Mental Health and Mental Subnormality (as it was then termed). In 1950 the role of the Psychiatric Nurse began to be recognised. In 1953 Schools of Nursing were instructed to include psychiatric experience in nurse training. In January 1959 the Nurse Training School at Dovenby opened with 10 students. There were two school intakes per year in January and May. The tutor at that time was Mr T Miller. Dr Ferguson gave lectures in Psychiatry. As he was also a JP in Cockermouth at the time, students were invited to observe court proceedings as patients were often admitted to Dovenby via the courts.

The training syllabus included:

- The Human Body - Anatomy and Physiology etc.
- Tray and trolley setting for various medical procedures
- Temperature, pulse, respiration and blood pressure recording
- Urine testing
- Drugs – administration and side effects
- Record keeping
- Diet
- Leisure activities
- Care of keys (Some wards were still being locked!)
- General nursing care – bed making, washing, prevention of pressure sores
- Care of the dying - Last Offices

Practical, written and oral examinations were taken at Prudhoe Hospital. Students in training observed a patient having Electro Convulsive Therapy (ECT) and were also taken to visit Garlands Hospital at Carlisle.

Student nurses wore white dresses with a bib piped with purple and a purple collar and belt.

Enrolled nurses wore uniforms piped with maroon. Staff nurses wore the same dresses piped with blue, deputy ward sisters' dresses were piped with green while ward sisters wore dresses piped with navy. All wore white caps. Male nurses wore a white coat with the colour on the collar denoting their status. In 1959 a former nurse recalls that her wage after deductions was approximately £28 per month – non resident.

Cadet Nurses. Photos James Fisher

Female nurses' accommodation was in Dovenby Hall itself while the male nurses lived upstairs in Orchard House. The matron at that time was Miss McHugh. Her deputy was Miss Conway. Final exams were taken after three years and if successful the students qualified as R.N.M.S. – Registered Nurse for the Mentally Subnormal. There were no enrolled nurses at this time but there were cadet nurses who were too young to undertake training but gained valuable experience working on the wards and departments.

Training School 1960s. Back row L to R:- John Hetherington (Tutor), Howard Tolley, John Major, Margaret Lightfoot, Sister Haddon and Joan Merris. Front row L to R:- Tony Burnyeat, Margaret Conner, Jean Byers and Belle Hadley. Photo Belle Hadley

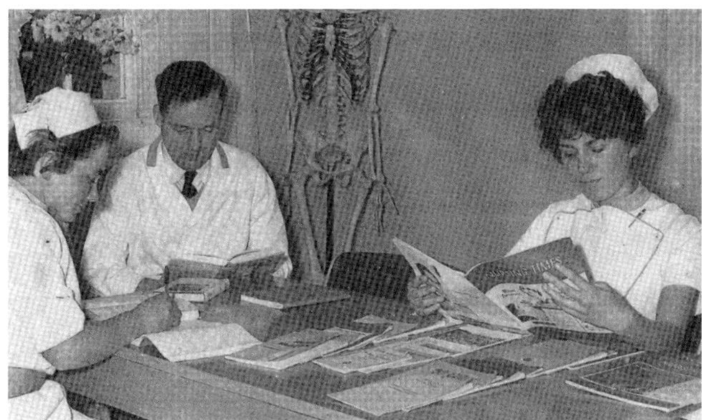

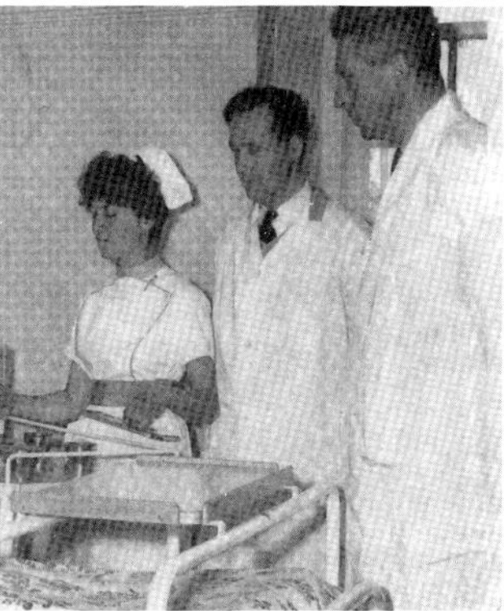

On the rounds. Above and right nurses during training at Dovenby Hall Hospital in 1961. Photo courtesy Cumbrian Newspapers

In the 1960s, in order to undertake training, student nurses first completed an application form, then attended the hospital for a medical examination followed by a test set by the General Nursing Council and formal interview prior to a six week induction course.

Mr Ronnie Brown commenced training in the second student intake in May 1959. When qualified he became a charge nurse on night duty. He then undertook training at West Cumberland Hospital for the general part of the register (SRN). After a short spell back at Dovenby he undertook the Clinical Nurse Teacher's course at Newcastle followed by a Registered Nurse Teacher's course at Carlisle and Huddersfield Polytechnic where he gained a Certificate of Education, thus enabling him to become a tutor at Dovenby, where he remained until training ceased in 2000.

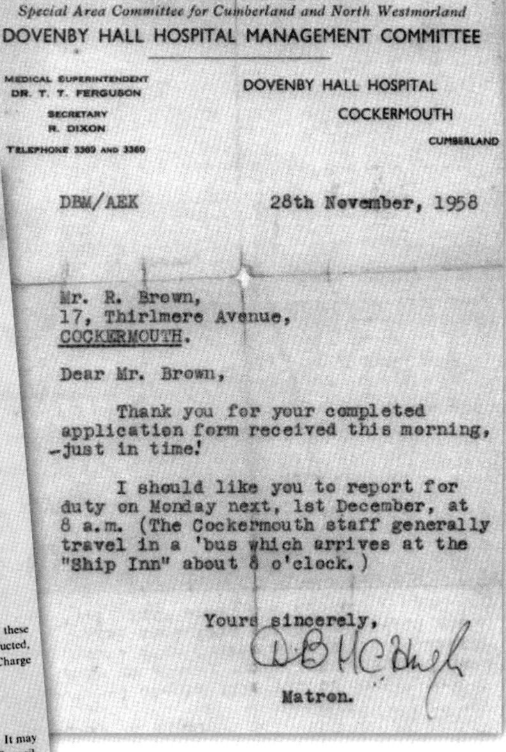

Newcastle Regional Hospital Board
Special Area Committee for Cumberland and North Westmorland

DOVENBY HALL HOSPITAL MANAGEMENT COMMITTEE

MEDICAL SUPERINTENDENT
DR. T. T. FERGUSON

SECRETARY
R. DIXON

TELEPHONE 3359 AND 3360

DOVENBY HALL HOSPITAL
COCKERMOUTH
CUMBERLAND

DBM/AEK

28th November, 1958

Mr. R. Brown,
17, Thirlmere Avenue,
COCKERMOUTH.

Dear Mr. Brown,

Thank you for your completed application form received this morning, -just in time!

I should like you to report for duty on Monday next, 1st December, at 8 a.m. (The Cockermouth staff generally travel in a 'bus which arrives at the "Ship Inn" about 8 o'clock.)

Yours sincerely,

D B McC[illegible]

Matron.

The General Nursing Council for England and Wales

Record of Practical Instruction and Experience for the Certificate of Mental Deficiency Nursing

Name of Student Nurse RONALD BROWN

Date of entry to training 4th. May 1959.

Index Number 231230

The Sister or Charge Nurse, as the various items are taught, is requested to mark these in the appropriate column; one stroke (/) to signify that the student nurse has been instructed, but is not yet proficient, a X to signify that the student is proficient. The Sister or Charge Nurse will sign the Record in the appropriate column wherever a X is marked.

Further copies of this publication may be obtained from the offices of the Council. It may not be re-printed or re-produced either in whole or in part without the sanction of the Council.

Records of practical training kindly contributed by Ronnie Brown

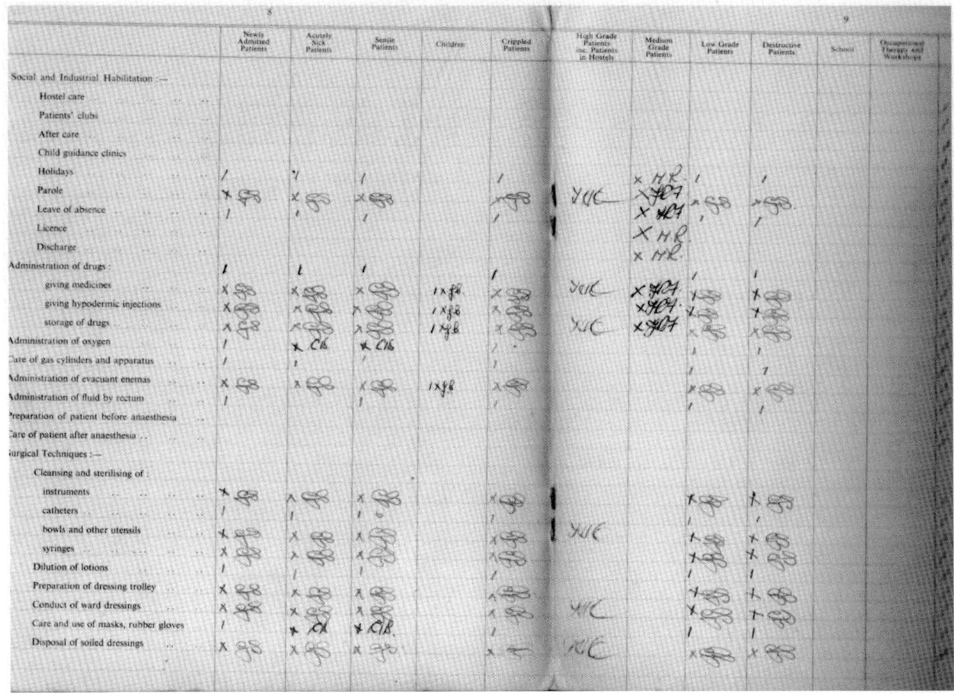

	Newly Admitted Patients	Acutely Sick Patients	Senile Patients	Children	Crippled Patients	High Grade Patients inc. Patients in Hostels	Medium Grade Patients	Low Grade Patients	Destructive Patients	School	Occupational Therapy and Workshops
Social and Industrial Habilitation :—											
Hostel care											
Patients' clubs											
After care											
Child guidance clinics											
Holidays											
Parole											
Leave of absence											
Licence											
Discharge											
Administration of drugs :											
giving medicines											
giving hypodermic injections											
storage of drugs											
Administration of oxygen											
Care of gas cylinders and apparatus											
Administration of evacuant enemas											
Administration of fluid by rectum											
Preparation of patient before anaesthesia											
Care of patient after anaesthesia											
Surgical Techniques :—											
Cleansing and sterilising of :											
instruments											
catheters											
bowls and other utensils											
syringes											
Dilution of lotions											
Preparation of dressing trolley											
Conduct of ward dressings											
Care and use of masks, rubber gloves											
Disposal of soiled dressings											

Record of training

Nurses who passed their final exams in July 1964 were presented with their badges. Standing L to R:- R Brown, J Lowther, C Hodgson, Mrs W Graham, J Carr, J R Rogers. Seated:- Mrs D Hetherington, Mrs H Dawson, Dr T T Ferguson, Mrs J G Jamieson (who presented the awards), Matron Miss B Conway and Nurse M Smith (Photo courtesy Cumbrian Newspapers)

Dovenby Hospital badge. Photo Peter Davey

GNC badge. Photo Peter Davey

Training took three years. Intermediate exams were taken after one year, practical exams at Prudhoe and written exams at Dovenby. £40 was paid on passing this exam and £50 on passing the final exams.

In 1994 the training school had 12 places for RMNS student nurses and 6 SEN pupil nurses. SEN training was two years. There were 12 places for cadets to help with recruitment.

Although the basic training in the 1970s and 1980s was almost unchanged, many extra courses and qualifications were introduced. Fire Training, Challenging Behaviour Courses and Child and Adolescent Psychiatric Nursing were examples of these.

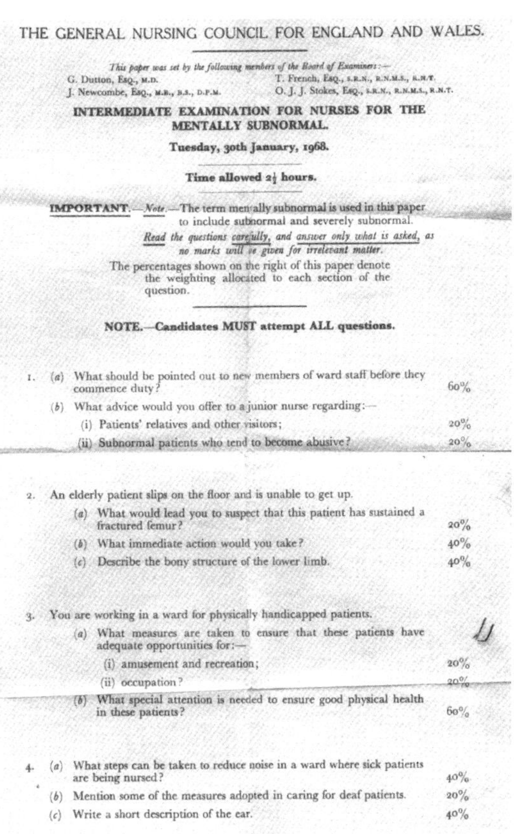

THE GENERAL NURSING COUNCIL FOR ENGLAND AND WALES.

This paper was set by the following members of the Board of Examiners:—

G. Dutton, Esq., M.D. — T. French, Esq., S.R.N., R.N.M.S., R.N.T.
J. Newcombe, Esq., M.B., B.S., D.P.M. — O. J. J. Stokes, Esq., S.R.N., R.N.M.S., R.N.T.

INTERMEDIATE EXAMINATION FOR NURSES FOR THE MENTALLY SUBNORMAL.

Tuesday, 30th January, 1968.

Time allowed 2½ hours.

IMPORTANT.—*Note.*—The term mentally subnormal is used in this paper to include subnormal and severely subnormal.

Read the questions carefully, and answer only what is asked, as no marks will be given for irrelevant matter.

The percentages shown on the right of this paper denote the weighting allocated to each section of the question.

NOTE.—Candidates MUST attempt ALL questions.

1. (*a*) What should be pointed out to new members of ward staff before they commence duty? 60%
   (*b*) What advice would you offer to a junior nurse regarding:—
   (i) Patients' relatives and other visitors; 20%
   (ii) Subnormal patients who tend to become abusive? 20%

2. An elderly patient slips on the floor and is unable to get up.
   (*a*) What would lead you to suspect that this patient has sustained a fractured femur? 20%
   (*b*) What immediate action would you take? 40%
   (*c*) Describe the bony structure of the lower limb. 40%

3. You are working in a ward for physically handicapped patients.
   (*a*) What measures are taken to ensure that these patients have adequate opportunities for:—
   (i) amusement and recreation; 20%
   (ii) occupation? 20%
   (*b*) What special attention is needed to ensure good physical health in these patients? 60%

4. (*a*) What steps can be taken to reduce noise in a ward where sick patients are being nursed? 40%
   (*b*) Mention some of the measures adopted in caring for deaf patients. 20%
   (*c*) Write a short description of the ear. 40%

Right: An example of an Intermediate examination paper

Below left and right: Registered Nurse Certificate

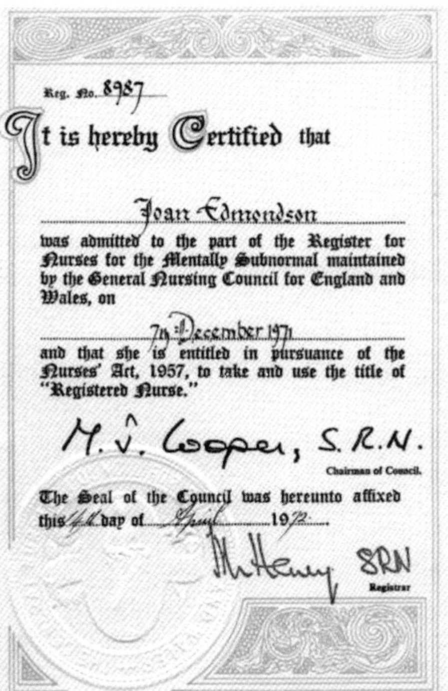

Reg. No. 8987

It is hereby Certified that

Joan Edmondson

was admitted to the part of the Register for Nurses for the Mentally Subnormal maintained by the General Nursing Council for England and Wales, on

7th December 1971

and that she is entitled in pursuance of the Nurses' Act, 1957, to take and use the title of "Registered Nurse."

M. J. Cooper, S.R.N.
Chairman of Council.

The Seal of the Council was hereunto affixed this 4th day of April 1972.

SRN
Registrar

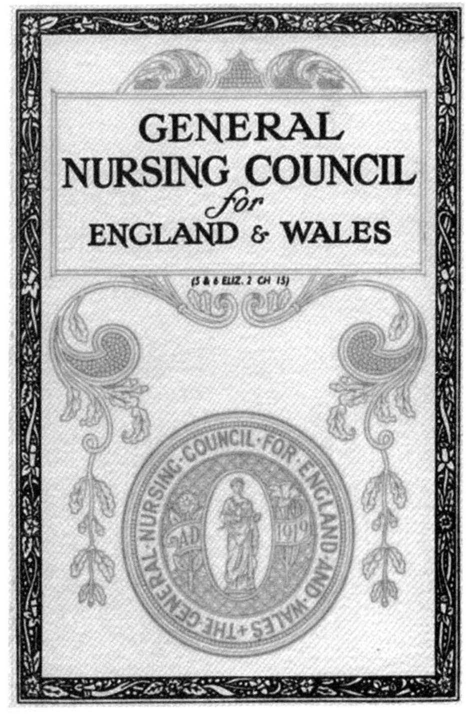

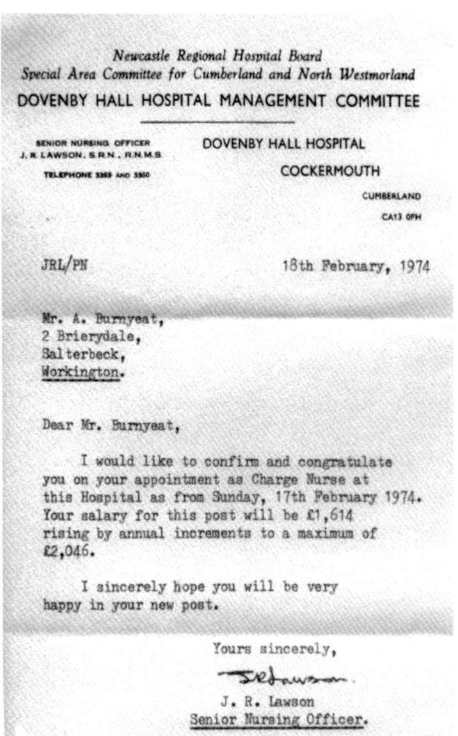

Newcastle Regional Hospital Board
Special Area Committee for Cumberland and North Westmorland
DOVENBY HALL HOSPITAL MANAGEMENT COMMITTEE

SENIOR NURSING OFFICER
J. R. LAWSON, S.R.N., R.N.M.S.
TELEPHONE 5369 AND 5500

DOVENBY HALL HOSPITAL
COCKERMOUTH
CUMBERLAND
CA13 0PH

JRL/PN

18th February, 1974

Mr. A. Burnyeat,
2 Brierydale,
Salterbeck,
Workington.

Dear Mr. Burnyeat,

I would like to confirm and congratulate you on your appointment as Charge Nurse at this Hospital as from Sunday, 17th February 1974. Your salary for this post will be £1,614 rising by annual increments to a maximum of £2,046.

I sincerely hope you will be very happy in your new post.

Yours sincerely,

J. R. Lawson
Senior Nursing Officer.

Note the wages for an experienced trained nurse in the 1970s

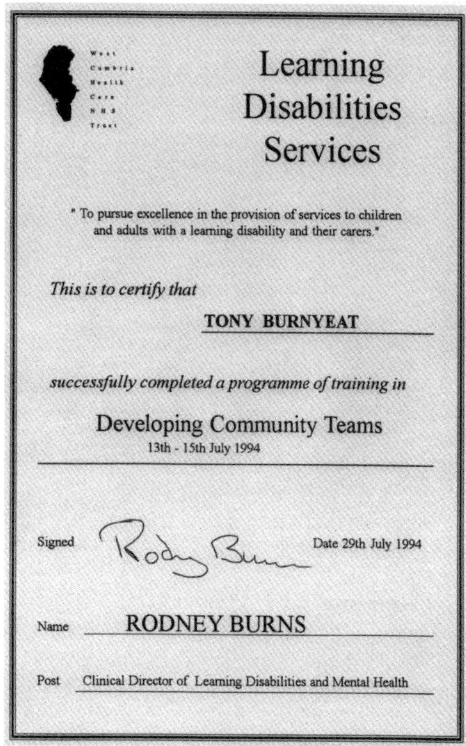

West Cumbria Health Care NHS Trust

Learning Disabilities Services

" To pursue excellence in the provision of services to children and adults with a learning disability and their carers."

This is to certify that

TONY BURNYEAT

successfully completed a programme of training in

Developing Community Teams
13th - 15th July 1994

Signed Date 29th July 1994

Name RODNEY BURNS

Post Clinical Director of Learning Disabilities and Mental Health

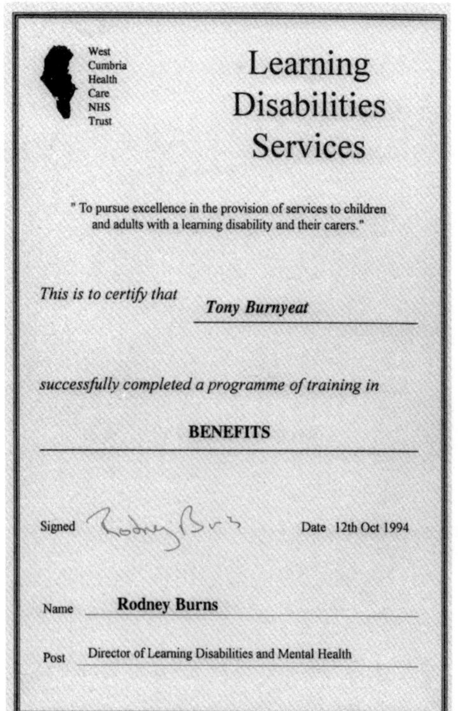

West Cumbria Health Care NHS Trust

Learning Disabilities Services

" To pursue excellence in the provision of services to children and adults with a learning disability and their carers."

This is to certify that *Tony Burnyeat*

successfully completed a programme of training in

BENEFITS

Signed Date 12th Oct 1994

Name Rodney Burns

Post Director of Learning Disabilities and Mental Health

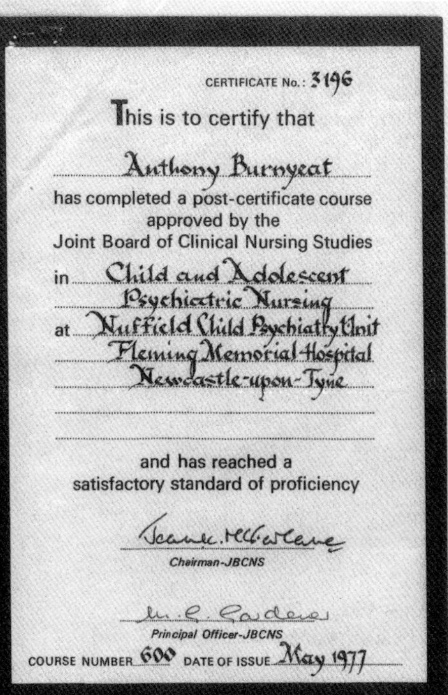

CERTIFICATE No.: 3196

This is to certify that

Anthony Burnyeat

has completed a post-certificate course approved by the Joint Board of Clinical Nursing Studies

in Child and Adolescent Psychiatric Nursing

at Nuffield Child Psychiatry Unit Fleming Memorial Hospital Newcastle-upon-Tyne

and has reached a satisfactory standard of proficiency

Chairman-JBCNS

Principal Officer-JBCNS

COURSE NUMBER 600 DATE OF ISSUE May 1977

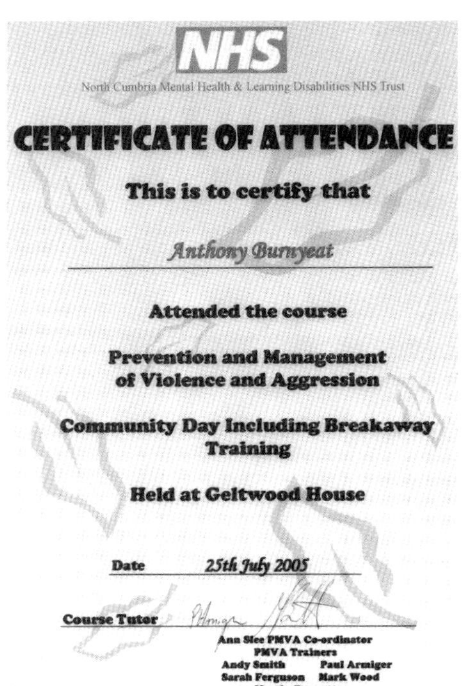

NHS
North Cumbria Mental Health & Learning Disabilities NHS Trust

CERTIFICATE OF ATTENDANCE

This is to certify that

Anthony Burnyeat

Attended the course

Prevention and Management
of Violence and Aggression

Community Day Including Breakaway
Training

Held at Geltwood House

Date 25th July 2005

Course Tutor

Ann Slee PMVA Co-ordinator
PMVA Trainers
Andy Smith Paul Armiger
Sarah Ferguson Mark Wood
Martin Bennett

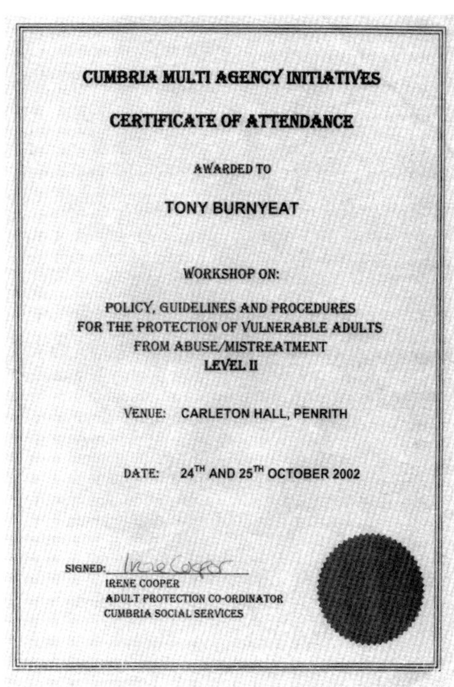

CUMBRIA MULTI AGENCY INITIATIVES

CERTIFICATE OF ATTENDANCE

AWARDED TO

TONY BURNYEAT

WORKSHOP ON:

POLICY, GUIDELINES AND PROCEDURES
FOR THE PROTECTION OF VULNERABLE ADULTS
FROM ABUSE/MISTREATMENT
LEVEL II

VENUE: CARLETON HALL, PENRITH

DATE: 24TH AND 25TH OCTOBER 2002

SIGNED: Irene Cooper
IRENE COOPER
ADULT PROTECTION CO-ORDINATOR
CUMBRIA SOCIAL SERVICES

In the 1980s other training courses included:

1988 – Step/Life Planning

1989 – Action Centred Leadership

Counselling courses

Code of Professional Conduct

Professional Clinical Development

Coping with potentially violent individuals

At this time the training school was still in Orchard House, on the main road, opposite the Ship Inn. As well as Ronnie Brown, other tutors included Bernard Ogden, Janet Major and Moira McDonald. Placements in Wigton and various day centres were included in the training.

In the 1990s legislation decreed a change in the exam procedure. There were no longer any practical exams and assessments were carried out during the last year of training. All exams were taken at Dovenby.

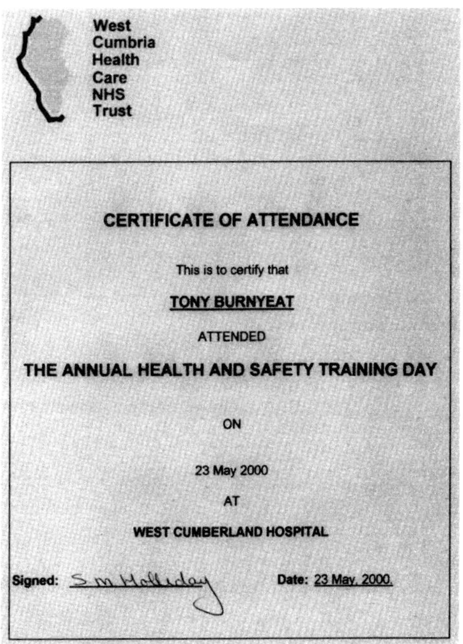

West
Cumbria
Health
Care
NHS
Trust

CERTIFICATE OF ATTENDANCE

This is to certify that

TONY BURNYEAT

ATTENDED

THE ANNUAL HEALTH AND SAFETY TRAINING DAY

ON

23 May 2000

AT

WEST CUMBERLAND HOSPITAL

Signed: S M Halliday Date: 23 May. 2000.

Certificates and information kindly contributed by Tony Burnyeat.

A TYPICAL DAILY ROUTINE ON AN ELDERLY CARE WARD IN THE 1960s

On a ward with 40 residents there would usually be 4 members of staff working a 12 hour shift (1 hour for lunch and ½ an hour for tea)

8.00am	Take over from night staff. Verbal report of night's events. Visual check on all residents. Check keys. Sign report.
8.15am	Allocate staff to duties. Residents' breakfasts - assist where required. Medicine round.
8.45-11.45am	Toilet round. Ensure residents attending therapies are clean and tidy and escort to same. Ensure all other residents are clean and tidy for the day. Bathing as per rota. Those residents confined to bed attended to. Mattresses washed and beds made as required. Doctors' rounds. Morning coffee. Individual programmes carried out i.e. continence care, mobility, prompts and training. Collect residents from therapies. Toilet round.
12-12.30pm	Lunch – assisting when required and carrying out individual feeding programmes. Medicine round.
12.30-2.30pm	Staff lunches.
1.30pm	Residents return to therapies. Ward activities – shopping trips – walks - minibus outings. Case conferences as required (all residents had a regular case review). Ward visitors – relatives or volunteers.
2.45pm	Tea and biscuits. Toilet round.
3.45pm	Residents return from therapies.
4.30pm	Tea time. Medicine round. Toilet round.
5.15pm	Social time – TV – chat – cards – dominoes – jigsaws – crochet – knitting.
7.30pm	Medicine round. Toilet round.
7.45pm	Hand over to night staff.

Specialist training courses were organised by the Learning Disability Service.

- Training in Benefits
- Negotiating Skills
- Interview Techniques
- Developing Community Teams
- Mental Health Awareness Course
- Health and Safety
- Raising Awareness in the Community

The term "Matron" was no longer used. Senior staff were referred to as Nursing Officers.

After the introduction of Project 2000, all training at Dovenby was transferred to the St Martin's College site at the West Cumberland Hospital, Hensingham.

Members of Dovenby staff who undertook the Rampton Hospital course in techniques of control and restraint receive thier certificates. Photo courtesy Cumbrian Newspapers

CHAPTER 6
REFLECTIONS

A DOCTOR'S MEMORIES OF DOVENBY HALL HOSPITAL

Naomi Kerr

My husband (George Kerr - born Whitehaven 1935 - school Whitehaven Grammar School) and I lived at Dovenby from September 1962 - January 1964. George had a junior doctor's job at Dovenby (which enabled him to attend as day release the Diploma in Psychiatric Medicine course at Newcastle University Medical School). We lived in a hospital owned house, one of 6 almost identical social housing type semis in a cul de sac adjacent to the extensive grounds around Dovenby House (the Medical Superintendent's house). We rented the house from the hospital for a subsidised rental. My memory of it was that it was very cold - the only means of heating was an open coal fire in the sitting room. The hospital had various other less modern cottages within the grounds and just outside the gates of the estate at the further end of the village. All these houses were rented by hospital employees and maintained by the engineering department of the hospital. This was normal practice for psychiatric and mental handicap hospitals at least up until the early 1980s when Dovenby Hospital real estate was sold off to private buyers.

Dovenby House (a large four square Cumbrian Georgian house lived in by the Medical Superintendent - in 1960 Dr Tom Ferguson) was surrounded by a field (now a modern housing estate) and in Dr Ferguson's time his daughter Nina had her two ponies in this field. In earlier times (i.e. 1930s and 1940s) one large part of this field had been devoted to the growing of rhubarb! Some nursing staff also had quarters in the old hall.

My husband's duties as junior doctor were to look after the physical health of the patients (residents) much as a GP would do, and also to look after the psychiatric health of the residents. He also had to be 'in charge' when Dr Ferguson was away - I cannot remember that there was any other senior cover when Dr Ferguson was away. Obviously some of the residents were troubled mentally - some as a result of whatever brain damage may have led to their mental handicap, and some as a result of the problems of institutionalisation, which was an understandable all pervading problem in the large isolated and isolating institutions of the early to mid 20th century. So informal were systems that I was able to help out on the wards even though I wasn't employed there - imagine the legal and health and safety implications of that happening now! I remember the wards being very crowded. Patients had almost no personal possessions nor anywhere to store them and I think were often dressed in other people's clothes. In particular I remember male wards where beds were touching each other and one might have to climb over other beds to get to examine someone ill in bed. In this situation it is not surprising there was an outbreak of TB. I think that at this period (early 1960s) there were about 380-420 residents - but I presume there are records that can verify this.

Residents/patients came into Dovenby for a variety of reasons. Indeed in 1962 several residents had been at the hospital since it opened in the 1930s (I think as a local authority facility, then presumably being given hospital status at the inception of the health service).

These are the reasons/sources from which residents came in the 40s 50s and 60s:

From the workhouse (1930s) presumably children from the workhouse who were considered to have too limited an intellectual capacity to be able to hold down paid employment.

From the courts - there were residents who had committed physically violent acts (usually against family members). They were judged unfit through mental handicap to plead and were in Dovenby often under a draconian mental health order (section 60), which meant they were virtually prisoners at Dovenby. There were also chronically offending petty criminals - judged to be of limited intellect, but really very cunning and they also came under mental health order. People under mental health orders were not allowed outside the hospital grounds without a member of staff and some perceived as gratuitously violent or dangerous were kept in locked wards. Modern views would I think be that most of these people could have led a less constrained life.

People admitted for largely spurious reasons - obviously handicapped children with genetic abnormalities whose parents were advised by doctors to 'put them away' and forget about them, and then older people who were admitted for largely social reasons in that their carers died or became too frail to care for them, or the handicapped person who developed challenging behaviour which made it difficult for their carers to manage.

I think it is worth remembering that there was no social funding at that time (as there is just about today), no Attendance Allowance, no Mobility Allowance, and no schooling for severely handicapped children, so that particularly for less well off people residential care of people with challenging handicaps may have seemed the only solution.

In 1960 Dovenby was a very self contained community with a rigidly hierarchical structure.

There were the STAFF and the PATIENTS, each were dependant on the other but there were rigid unspoken rules about behaviour.

On the staff side there was the Medical Superintendent (Dr Ferguson - a Scotsman) who together with his wife (who I think ran the hospital pharmacy - her family having had pharmaceutical interests in Scotland) formed an almost royalty like position. They had permanent household help from a resident (this was entirely normal practice in mental hospitals until mid 70s). They lived in Dovenby House where their rent would have been subsidised but when there was no junior resident doctor Dr Ferguson would have been on call 24/7. He had the oak panelled room as his consulting room in the main hall, with a notice on the door reading MEDICAL SUPERINTENDENT.

Then there was the matron who lived in a roomy, not to say, grand flat at the front of the 1st floor of the Hall. She had 2 residents acting as her maids. I remember spending Christmas Day 1963 at her flat together with the Fergusons and we were served with an amazingly grand meal!

The 3rd important person was the hospital administrator. He would have been responsible for the non clinical staff, buildings etc. but I am afraid I can't remember anything about him.

The hospital was self sufficient in building maintenance, grounds maintenance, laundry, sewing (curtains etc and some patient's clothes alterations etc and probably nurses' uniforms). Patients helped in these departments.

Those patients who didn't help in the day to day maintenance/running of the hospital (for which they would have received a very small sum - less than £1/week - but then the weekly wage for an unskilled worker would not have been much over £10 at that time) might be occupied in the occupational therapy department. There, there were occasional contracts to do, simple assembly of stuff for local firms, sticks were chopped and sold in paper sacks, and coir mats were made in an incredibly skilful manner. Simple embroidery was also done.

Patient entertainment centred on the 'rec' - a hall at the front of the grounds - there films were shown and there were dances - which staff also attended though staff and residents would not have danced together.

"Beds were touching each other and one might have to climb over other beds to get to examine someone."

Former Recreation Hall today. Photo Maureen Fisher

Extracts from Dr George Kerr's obituary which appeared in the 'Psychiatric Bulletin' B.M.J. in 1992.

GEORGE KERR, formerly Consultant Psychiatrist and Medical Administrator, Dovenby Hall Hospital, Cockermouth, Cumbria and Director of the National Development Team for Mentally Handicapped People.

Dr George Kerr died aged 56 on August 3rd 1991 from multiple sclerosis which had dogged his professional career and forced his early retirement in 1986. A founder member of the College, he was elected to the Fellowship in 1980.

George entered the field of mental handicap at a period of great change. He was a passionate believer in modern philosophies and a champion of normalisation, care in the community and teamwork – goals he worked tirelessly to achieve in his clinical posts and in his work at the Department of Health and Social Security. Caring and sensitive and with a quiet energy, he had little difficulty in carrying staff with him. He pioneered the resettlement of residents from Dovenby Hall Hospital into the integrated community care programmes based on small homes and community teams.

He received his medical training at Bristol University and Medical School and after early jobs in medicine and neurology he entered psychiatry in 1962 as a Junior Hospital Medical Officer at Dovenby followed by registrar training in hospitals in the north east.

His first consultant post was at Earl's House Hospital, Durham (1968-71) where he oversaw an extensive modernisation and rebuilding programme.

In 1971 he was appointed Senior Lecturer in the Department of Psychiatry at Southampton University and Consultant Psychiatrist to Coldeast Hospital, Southampton. From 1973 he also held a part-time appointment as Specialist Advisor in Mental Handicap to the Department of Health and Social Security which involved him in a punishing schedule of daily commuting.

He returned to Dovenby as Consultant Psychiatrist and Medical Administrator in 1975 where, over the next ten years he set about modernising services for the mentally handicapped in East and West Cumbria.

From 1975 to 1977 he was a member of the Jay Committee on Nursing and the Care of the Mentally Handicapped and in 1984 he became Director of the National Development Team for Mentally Handicapped. Sadly, failing health forced him to retire from this post after only nine months and shortly afterwards from professional work altogether.

He bore his illness, which began when he was a medical student with great courage and fortitude.

He is survived by his wife, Naomi, a general practitioner in Cumbria, who provided untiring support throughout his career, and their two children whose achievements and individuality gave him much pride and pleasure.

Contributed by Kenneth Day

VOLUNTEERS AT DOVENBY

Mrs R Thom-Postlethwaite

In spite of the country being just about bankrupt after WWII, followed by the Korean War, which made things even worse, Dovenby Hall Hospital, which was running on a shoestring budget, had a tremendous reputation locally. I used to hear it being referred to as "that wonderful place which has done wonders for so and so". The staff were amazing, working in pretty primitive conditions, with patients kept in locked wards but well fed, warm and clean.

When I joined the Management Committee in 1960 things were looking up. The wards were left unlocked and new drugs were coming onto the market so that any severely disturbed patients could be contained without being locked up. There was a feeling of optimism and the patients were cheerful, friendly and on the whole happy considering that they were excluded from the real world. I determined to bring the real world to them.

The management committee allowed me, as a WVS organiser, to open a coffee shop and a village type shop so that the patients had somewhere "normal" to go to spend their pocket money and meet their friends from other wards. This proved very popular with both patients and staff. We sold cigarettes, sweets, biscuits, toiletries and some clothing and to begin with we were open seven days a week bringing in teams of volunteers from other organisations as well as our own to help man the place. We soon learned that, mentally handicapped or not, some of the patients were very quick witted – rather more than us sometimes! Fizzy drinks went down very well and they got through so many that our shop was a bit short of space, so the empty boxes were put outside at the back for collection. The patients were given a penny if they returned empty bottles which they did in a steady stream all day long until someone spotted them helping themselves to the empties round the back! Keys could not be left out for a moment or they vanished but the patients behaved beautifully and we had no trouble getting volunteers. At one time we had two female doctors and a senior nurse on our list. It was all good fun. Dr Ferguson gave us good support and his successor, Dr Short, had ideas of opening one or two more little shops so that the village people could come in to Dovenby for items such as groceries and shoe repairs thus bringing the public into the hospital rather than sending the patients out into the community where there were no facilities for them. "Higher Grade" patients liked to be sent out but there was little for them to do except hang around on street corners whereas at Dovenby there were all sorts of activities and training available.

There was an excellent hall for dances with a stage at one end and an altar set up behind curtains at the other end which was used for church services for all denominations. Mass was celebrated at 4pm on Sundays and members of the Catholic faith from the wider community were invited to attend. The patients loved to attend church services, particularly the hymn singing. They sang the tunes with gusto but some were often heard to be singing the words of nursery rhymes which they knew off by heart!

By the 1970s overcrowding was still a big problem but building work went on and several new wards had been put up – and one burnt down one very hot day when the windows were left open and a patient, with an illegal box of matches, set fire to the curtains. It is easy to understand the temptation there was because the usual calm was shattered by the arrival of lovely red fire engines with bells ringing and everyone rushing about – a nice change to the normal routine!

Dovenby League of Friends fundraising 1970s. Photo courtesy Cumbrian Newspapers

Photos Pat Tyson

Mrs Pat Tyson introduced riding for the disabled which was very popular. We broke all the rules of the Riding for the Disabled Society who stipulated that horses should not be taken into a "mental institution" but it was the only way to reach the more profoundly disabled who really needed to take part. Girls from Cockermouth Grammar School gave us real support and raised a lot of money for us at a time when the BBC were offering us money to build a pony shelter, but only if we could match their donation. I shall never forget seeing a little boy, who was so disabled he had to lie on the floor all day as he couldn't sit up, being laid flat on a pony's back and being taken out into the sunshine with a girl either side to hold him on. He couldn't speak but as soon as he felt the sunshine his little face lit up. Eventually he was able to sit up on the horse and become stronger.

A Friends of Dovenby Hospital organisation was formed and they raised money for a therapy pool, but not long after it was built the hospital closed.

By this time patients were known as residents and as many as possible went to live in hostels or flats under the supervision of Social Services. This was great for most of them but hard on the older residents who had lived in Dovenby all their lives and felt it was their home.

At Dovenby they had their own old people's club – the Eventide Club - where elderly residents knitted squares to be made into blankets for Ethiopia which they learned all about from the television.

My own chief memories are of feeling tremendous admiration for the fortitude of the patients, many of whom had to endure severe handicaps both mental and physical all their lives and the wonderful nurses who looked after them so cheerfully and kindly in spite of often having to work in far from ideal conditions. Money was always a problem, so much was needed.

It was a privilege to try to help.

Dovenby Hall Management Committee (Disbanded 1974). Back Row L to R:- Jim Lawson (Senior Nursing Officer), Dr Elderkin,(Consultant Paediatrician), Dr Short (Consultant Psychiatrist), Dr P T Griffith(Consultant Ophthalmologist), Mr Norman Kirkby (Hospital Treasurer) and Mr Fawcett. Front Row L to R:- Mr Reg Dixon, Mrs Thom-Postlethwaite, Mrs Shepherd (Chairman), Mrs Clarabelle St John Curwen and Mr Long. Photo contributed by Dr P T Griffith

Eppie Gibson was cycling home from rugby practise one evening at dusk.

As he passed Dovenby a voice from over the perimeter wall called "Goodnight", which gave him such a fright he almost fell off!

A PHYSIOTHERAPIST'S MEMORY OF DOVENBY

Johnny Sealby

Joining the staff at Dovenby Hall in 1971, as their first physiotherapist, introduced me to a new world so different from my 26 years experience of work in ordinary hospitals. Dovenby was a residential establishment for the "educationally challenged", which was staffed by doctors, nurses, maintenance and clerical staff.

It also had a visiting dentist and others with special interests.

In its large grounds was a "special Local Education Authority school" for its own children. Dovenby functioned more like a thriving village than an "asylum" – old terminology.

However, changes were already afoot in the nursing profession generally and the dark clouds of dissolution that would destroy this happy village were gathering ominously. I wondered what the staff would make of my appointment, for they were naturally aware of the new ideas hatched by enthusiasts with the best of intentions, of course, but little understanding of the facts and consequences.

I needn't have worried. The staff were generous with help. The tutors in our Training School for nurses advised on text books to banish my ignorance of mental disorders, and I was tutored by a wonderful Staff Nurse seconded temporarily to my one-man-band. So we set off to visit all the wards or rather houses scattered round the grounds, and later included the children's school and occupational department, which was run by the nurses. Much of our time was spent with the children on the principle that the best results of treatment like those of education are gained by "catching 'em young".

Now the more profound the challenge to our residents educationally, the more difficult was it to communicate with them to the point where it seemed impossible. The answer was Behaviour Modification as practiced by the nurses. Very simply it is rewarding good or desired behaviour immediately with a recognisable form of approval. The physiotherapist has in her/his tool kit many techniques that can be used to predispose one's motor system to respond in a particular way. She/he can tap into tendon reflexes, use postural reactions or alert muscles by lightly brushing the skin over them, for example. Then by using appropriate combinations of these primitive neurological routes of "communication" we can, with the help of rewards, induce actions that can be built into activities, e.g. feeding or walking. This method should not be thought of as an imposition on a helpless individual any more than is the rewarding of a pupil with the sheer joy of achieving understanding of a difficult subject taught well by an enthusiastic teacher.

Later, cadet nurses were assigned to us for part of their training, which was most helpful especially when Dovenby was presented with a heated therapy pool. Everyone enjoyed it, and it was very good for treating spasticity and other disabilities. It was there I got my come-uppance. I preferred to go in the water wearing waders, as if going fishing instead of being in a swimming costume like everyone else. I said I'd be ready for any emergency. This, though, did not meet with my worthy "tutor's" approval. So I got a bucketful of pool water down the back of my waders, much to everyone's amusement.

After a while, my "tutor" returned to her nursing duties and an assistant joined the department in whose capable hands I could leave things while attending courses throughout the country on related subjects. Apart from furthering knowledge, it allowed the exchange of ideas and views on the state of affairs in our field with a variety of other interested professionals.

When a car and driver were made available visits to other establishments, special schools and individuals living at home became possible. These last were known to us through day care or short term stay. It was most interesting to see them with their parents in their own homes. One could learn about the parents' problems and demonstrate methods of dealing with them.

Near to Dovenby Hall is the market town of Cockermouth. I well remember walking along its main street and hearing the approach of unsteady steps, then the strangely articulated, though familiar, greeting as two strong arms enclosed me in a warm hug. He now lived in the town and recognised me from Dovenby. This was a real, unadulterated expression of humanity, to which I reciprocated unashamedly. Incidentally, although I was blind as a bat, I was never taken advantage of nor was I ever in danger.

Looking back now over my time at Dovenby till I retired in 1983, I can affirm that Dovenby was in the vanguard of those in the same field providing the most enlightened service to their recipients. When it is remembered that there was a huge range of ability (or disability) – from zero to just below the median – among our residents, this was a remarkable achievement. Certainly there were some at the top of the range who ought to be resettled in the community, but Dovenby had already done that. The complex conditions of those left behind, often compounded with physical disabilities, needed a high level of care and understanding of a specialised nature. Of course they needed exposure to the public by outings and the like, and visits from friends and relatives which they also got in abundance at Dovenby. They needed easy accessibility for those looking after them. They very much needed companionship (birds of a feather) and freedom to wander in safety. All this thcy had at Dovenby Hall.

What they do not need is to be trapped in small, uneconomic groups scattered around the county, where dedicated staff struggle to reach the former high standards of care. Nor do they need to be stuck in single accommodation among the public, where I have heard them say they were "lonely".

In other words what they really need is Dovenby Hall!

Dovenby functioned more like a thriving village than an "asylum".

The therapy pool can be seen behind the pavilion on the right of this aerial photo.

THE FIRST HOLIDAY 1965

James Fisher (1962 – 66)

Until 1965, it was not considered feasible for the residents to go on holiday unless relatives took them. However Brian Maguire, Deputy Matron, had persuaded the Management Committee to allow two groups to spend a few days away. I was told Mr Maguire wanted to see me and was summoned to his office. Although we had had our arguments in the past I couldn't think of anything I had done wrong on this particular occasion.

I was asked if I would accompany some of the male residents to Blackpool for three days, Wednesday to Friday. I was told that it would be in my own time. Thursday and Friday were my days off and I was told that it wouldn't be possible to give me any alternative days off.

I think it was (and I stand to be corrected if anyone knows differently) Sister Blaylock, Deputy Sister Marie Ann Hodgson and Lilian Chamberlain who left on the Monday, with a group of ladies from Patterson House. On Wednesday morning, Charge Nurse John Carr, Deputy Stan Stephenson and myself, at the time a third year student nurse, accompanied a group of men, mostly from Howard House and E2, to Blackpool. We arrived after lunch and as we disembarked the ladies were waiting to board the coach back to Dovenby.

We found ourselves billeted in a guest house not far from the tower. For a group of twenty seven to wander round Blackpool together would be difficult, so those who felt confident in making their own way

Outside hotel in Blackpool. Photo Belle Hadley

Photo James Fisher

around were able to do so. Where some of them got to, I don't know! We had booked a coach trip one afternoon and several of the residents were late for lunch and almost missed the trip. Bed time was delayed on Wednesday and Thursday nights as several had gone out for a walk after the cinema and hadn't returned. I had to walk to the South Shore and back looking for them. Isn't Blackpool dark when the illuminations are switched off? I remember on the Thursday night the police had been alerted and, as I was returning from my search from the South Shore direction with a few of the stragglers, picking up more on the way back, I was stopped by a constable who insisted on walking back to the guest house with us.

We stayed in Blackpool until after tea on the Friday. The coach picked us up at about 6.30pm so it was after 10pm when we got back to Dovenby. It was a very successful holiday marred only by the news on our return that Assistant Matron, Arthur Chandler, had died while we were away.

Joan Warwick, former nurse, remembers taking groups of residents to Blencathra which was once a sanatorium at Threlkeld, near Keswick, for holidays. Joan recalls that the food was excellent but that there wasn't a great deal for the residents to do and a week can feel like a month in those isolated surroundings!

WORKING AT DOVENBY HALL AS A STUDENT 1956-59

Barbara Kelly (née Burnett)

As I intended to train as a teacher, I was asked to work in the school at the hospital.

The children were of all ages, and of very limited ability, with only one teacher. I think some of them must have been brought in daily, although some of the older ones were full time residents. The 'teaching' was very basic, with lots of games and toys to help the children play. That was my first summer holiday work.

In subsequent years, my summer holidays were spent working there as a 'nurse'. The shifts were 8am until 8pm, with tea breaks and lunch provided in the staff canteen.

If the weather was fine, I cycled from Cockermouth but otherwise took the Maryport bus which stopped at Dovenby.

I had a family member, Peggy Logan, living in the Hospital in the ward where I worked. You can imagine the fuss she made when she knew I was on duty. Everyone had to be told of our relationship – distant cousins!

One of the less pleasant duties was bath time with the patients. There was a certain smell associated with them which was very noticeable when they were undressed for bathing. Some of the ladies were very obstreperous and rude, swearing and hitting out at others and staff. At these times the very difficult ones would be locked away, and treated with tranquilisers for a certain length of time. The more ambulant ladies were given jobs such as mopping floors, and general cleaning under our supervision.

The sister I remember in the women's ward was Sister Cahill, an Irish lady, a mixture of strictness and friendliness.

I also remember spending some time in the children's ward where children were just lying in padded cots all of the time. They had to be fed, washed, changed and turned in their cots while they made screaming and moaning noises. Obviously many of them were in Dovenby because their parents could not cope with them at home.

At weekends some of the patients had family and friends who visited them, but very few were taken out for any length of time.

My husband, Bill Kelly, remembers working at the same time as I was when we were courting in our student days. He worked on one of the male wards and found bath times difficult because some of the men were overweight and very heavy. So he used to walk some of them in the grounds for fresh air and exercise while they smoked and swore a great deal!

But we both acknowledge that conditions for this kind of patient have greatly improved over the 50 years since we experienced it, thanks to advances in medical and psychological care within the N.H.S..

JEAN BYERS' MEMORIES

Jean left school in 1937 at the age of 14 without any qualifications and worked in a baker's shop, then Walter Wilson's and later as a school cleaner. However, Jean had always wanted to be a nurse so when her younger child, Ann, started secondary school in 1962, she began working as an auxiliary nurse at Dovenby Hall Hospital. Jean was very bright so it wasn't long before Dr. Ferguson, the Medical Superintendent, noticed Jean and her way of working. He was very impressed by her proficiency and suggested that she should undergo training which she did over the next two years to become a State Enrolled Mental Handicap Nurse. After that, Dr. Ferguson wanted her to be able to take charge of wards so she trained as a State Registered Mental Handicap Nurse for the next two and a half years. Jean found the course fascinating and later was appointed Deputy Sister to Sister Jean Lothian.

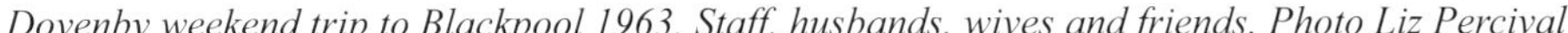

Dovenby weekend trip to Blackpool 1963. Staff, husbands, wives and friends. Photo Liz Percival

One 'patient' in particular Jean remembers was a lady who had been in the workhouse since she was tiny. She told Jean that in the workhouse they were always cold and hungry. This lady was unusual in that she could read any books she was given. Jean felt that perhaps Dovenby was perhaps not the right place for her but at least she was always warm and well fed.

When she first started as an Enrolled Nurse, Jean was paid £11 per month but was earning £600 per month when she retired in 1984.

"The residents used to call me Nurse By-byes. I always did what was asked of me and I loved the job."

When the hospital closed, Jean was asked to work part-time at the West Cumberland Hospital because she was qualified to administer injections and drugs. However, she decided to devote more time to her husband and grandchildren instead.

THE EVENTIDE CLUB

Edyth Stephenson

When the Eventide Club was formed the aim was to gather together the elderly residents from their various wards on one afternoon per week. Later, when a larger room was available, they were able to meet every day from 8.30am-12noon and from 1pm-4pm Monday to Friday.

Daily attendance could be between 20-30 each day.

On Mondays a lady called Mrs Banton from Flimby came to teach dancing which was much enjoyed and it was surprising how proficient the members became.

Thursday afternoon was concert practice time which gave a lot of pleasure to the members. They formed a concert party, travelling to various venues, including church halls, residential homes, hospitals and other over 60s' clubs to perform many well known songs. The choir won a cup at Carlisle Music Festival in the over 60s' category.

On Friday afternoons a group went along to join a painting class and produced some really good pictures which were displayed at an exhibition at St. Michael's Day Centre, Workington.

During the summer months outings were arranged, when the weather permitted, and holidays were organised to Blackpool and Scotland. Those who were unable to go on holiday were taken on trips to local areas such as Keswick, Silloth and St. Bees which invariably ended up with a fish and chip supper!

Visiting day, when families and friends could come and spend time with the residents, was on the first Saturday of the month. On these days the club opened to sell tea and biscuits, the proceeds from which went into club funds. It also provided a useful opportunity for staff to meet relatives.

The Eventide Club shop was set up for members so that they didn't have to queue in the main coffee shop. It eventually evolved into the main sweet shop which served all the residents.

When the main coffee shop closed due to lack of volunteers, the Eventide Club shop benefitted from the extra customers which increased profits and boosted club funds.

Visiting day, when family and friends could come and spend time with the residents, was the first Saturday in the month.

AWAKENING OF AN INNOCENT

Pauline Harkness (née Ostle)

My encounter with Dovenby Hall Hospital was brief but painful. When I was in the 6th form at Cockermouth Grammar School in 1956, I went along to the hospital to ask if they could give me a job during the summer holidays. I was told I could start the next day at 8am to work until 8pm with breaks for Camp coffee, lunch and tea and was given a white uniform.

My school friend Barbara Burnett from Cockermouth, was also given a job and we worked together for 6 days a week and then were given two or three days off. There was also another student from Workington Grammar School called Nancy Smith and we were all three intending to become teachers not nurses! For a 48 hour week we were paid £5 and glad of it.

I would rise at 7am and cycle from Greysouthen to Brigham, cross the railway line, (no A66 then) then the bridge over the Derwent at Broughton and ride along the narrow Craggs road until I reached the lower gate to Dovenby Hall grounds. I would cycle up through the woods, full of red squirrels and pheasants, to reach the main buildings. The weather was mainly fine in July and August (unlike now) and I managed to cycle home before dark.

I was a completely innocent 17 year old who had had a sheltered upbringing and what I saw in the hospital shocked me to the core. I had been completely unaware that our world contained unfortunate human beings who were abnormal in different ways. One experience which is etched on my memory was being told to bath an old lady called Margaret. Her physical deformity was revealed to me and I just swallowed hard and did as I was told. I was informed afterwards that the deformity could have been caused by an unsuccessful attempt to abort her.

As for staff, I remember from the meal breaks a Scottish lady, Sister Blair, who was very strict and also a genial male nurse called Jack Rogers from Broughton.

Although I valued this experience as part of my education for life, during the first week of my work there, I cried myself to sleep every night, so distressed did I feel for those unfortunate human beings.

"I had been completely unaware that our world contained unfortunate human beings who were abnormal in different ways."

CHAPTER 7
CHANGES

MEDICAL SUPERVISION

Terry Collins (Retired GP)
Clinical Assistant Dovenby Hall Hospital 1979 – 1996

In 1979 I was appointed, with two other doctors in Maryport Group Practice, to provide full general medical services to all residents of Dovenby Hall Hospital. This was the provision of the usual care expected from a general practitioner, mainly for physical illness. It did not include the specialist care provided by the Consultant Psychiatrists but as the remit involved providing 24 hour cover there was some overlap.

There had been more limited general practitioner cover and attendance by a doctor on three mornings a week on the hospital site. This regular work was allocated between the three doctors in the practice with clinical assistant appointments. The emergency and out of hours cover was undertaken by the practice on-call doctor. Another doctor in the practice attended the hospital on the other weekdays for specialist medical assessments but was often able to see residents with physical illness on those days.

An additional commitment in the contract was a full medical examination of all new admissions and discharges. Subsequently a regular annual full medical examination was undertaken on all residents and also the assessment of all residents who were to have a general anaesthetic for dental surgery in the dental suite on site. A Consultant Anaesthetist from West Cumberland Hospital attended for these lists.

In 1979 the residents at Dovenby had very mixed disabilities. Some had been admitted many years earlier in relatively good health, became older over time, but were essentially everyday patients for a GP with a normal range of illnesses. Other residents did have a spectrum of learning disability which made assessment more difficult if communication was impaired or there was a behaviour trait that made examination difficult – such as repetitive movements or walking around during examination.

The residents who had severe challenging behaviour were very difficult to assess as they frequently had multiple disabilities, were often strong young men and had communication problems. Initially children with mixed physical and learning difficulties were admitted to Dovenby who were again often difficult to assess, but who bore the most dreadful physical disabilities with extraordinary apparent cheerfulness. The observations of the nursing staff, who knew these residents well and who recognised the subtle changes in behaviour which indicated the start of illness, were a vital part of the assessment.

Emergency admissions to the West Cumberland Hospital were infrequent and when they occurred often caused distress and upset for the resident involved. However one of our responsibilities was the management of status epilepticus which was very worrying and serious. Many residents had associated epilepsy which was often complex and was managed by a multi-drug regime. A protocol was usually agreed for residents at risk with the administration of medication after consecutive fits. If this did not control the episodes, which were often very violent, on site assessment and treatment took place and then admission was often needed.

Dovenby grounds 1970s

Protocols were also occasionally agreed with consultants at Whitehaven over on site emergency treatment and, if necessary, admissions for residents who were difficult to assess and had symptoms such as recurrent severe abdominal pain. Although these distressing symptoms usually resolved spontaneously admission for observation was necessary if they were prolonged.

Many changes took place over the seventeen years in line with national policies. Some units closed and their residents were rehabilitated into the community. The admission of children was stopped and they were all placed in smaller support units. In 1979 there were large numbers of residents on each unit but these gradually reduced. In 1996 the hospital closed and the remaining residents were discharged very successfully to residential and nursing homes.

I took a number of memories with me when the Hospital closed, not least the beautiful grounds. I particularly remember the dedication of the staff and an awareness of the need to be very alert to concerns over minor changes, by those with intimate knowledge of the residents, and the need to observe carefully when conventional assessment is not possible. I especially remember the amazing fortitude of the children with multiple disabilities who were always so uncomplaining.

The observations of the nursing staff, who knew these residents well and who recognised the subtle changes in behaviour which indicated the start of illness, were a vital part of the assessment.

ALDINGHAM HALL

Tony Gilbert

In the 1970s there was a growing change of thinking regarding the care of people with learning disabilities, although in those days they were referred to as having a mental handicap. For many years a substantial number had been confined to institutions, notably hospitals. Caring for large numbers, often on overcrowded wards, meant that the notion of treating people as individuals, with their own unique needs, tended to be at best an aspiration, but in practice was unachievable. Similarly a person's need for dignity and privacy, taken for granted by most of us, was impossible to provide within a large institution. Sadly, people with a "mental handicap" were stigmatised and defined by their label. The concept that they had the capacity to develop was not widely recognised. Furthermore there were those living in hospitals who should never have been placed there, but once there found it impossible to leave.

A dramatic change in the situation was imminent and proposals were outlined in a Government White Paper "Better Services for the Mentally Handicapped" in 1971.

The plan was that there should be a move from a service based on a hospital/medical model to one with a community base. The concept underlying the changes was that of normalisation. People with a learning disability did not require medical care, beyond that of the general population. Basically their needs were social. Life in the community would broaden horizons and offer wider opportunities, previously denied. There was the prospect of employment for some, a home of their own, better social and leisure opportunities and a greater control over their lives. A more personal service was envisaged, recognising a person's individuality and worth. The person with the learning disability would be at the centre of the service and their views and aspirations recognised. In addition to "Better Services", the ideas of the National Development Team (comprising leading figures in the field), also guided developments.

Although this was an exciting prospect for many, it was a frightening one for others. For all those years spent in hospital, people with a "mental handicap" did not have to worry about making choices and decisions were made for them. There was security. Consequently it was clear that if a widespread transfer from hospital to the community was going to be successful, adequate services needed to set up to support people through such a major change. In 1978 the opening of Aldingham Hall was the first step.

Previously the record of the Local Authorities and the Health Service working together had not always been successful. This project depended on cooperation. Funds were allocated on a joint financing basis. A joint care planning team was set up to help develop services and maintain an oversight. Aldingham Hall was the product of joint Health and Local Authority funding.

Once the funding was in place you might think the way was clear to proceed. It was not as simple as that. Aldingham Hall is set in the small village of Aldingham, in a rural area, on the shores of Morecambe Bay. Amongst its residents there was widespread fear about the impact of the change of use of the Hall. In short there was fierce opposition. At one point the Bishop of Carlisle had to step in to assert the church's backing for the project, a much needed proclamation of support. Huge efforts were made by key figures to change public perception. Fear of the unknown was the predominant factor. Happily, in time, the hostility subsided, and indeed, transformed into support. The parish council gave its approval, and the local vicar, who had initially opposed the opening, in time, was convinced of the value of the service. Indeed, at a later date, he even agreed to officiate at the wedding of two ex Dovenby Hall residents, who at the time were living at Aldingham Hall, a good example of normalisation in practice. Much effort was put into developing good relations with the community, including employing local people, where appropriate.

So, after this major battle, Aldingham Hall opened. Extensive work was still needed to be done in winning support. Relatives of residents were uneasy. For years they had seen the hospital as a secure long term care solution. Often they were sceptical, anxious and apprehensive about the proposed changes. Existing carers were unhappy and fearful for the future for the residents they had been caring for. Residents themselves needed to see that a move would be in their interests, but in the end would they be prepared to take a step into the unknown? One might think that years of living in an institution would have led to a strong resistance to change. Naturally there was an extensive preparation programme, meetings, and visits to Aldingham Hall. In obtaining volunteers there was an awareness of the need to avoid putting pressure on people. The aim was to enable them to make their own informed choice. As it happens there was never any difficulty finding volunteers, and, in all, three hundred people used the service. Not all were from Dovenby Hall, as people were also invited from the community, local authority hostels and from the Royal Albert Hospital in Lancaster.

The primary aim of Aldingham Hall was to help people in the transition from hospital to the community, to develop independence in accordance with their potential, and to equip them for life outside the hospital. Attention was given to the development of life skills and social skills. Educational and social opportunities needed to be offered. Building confidence was an important element, given that low expectations and stigmatisation had inevitably undermined confidence and self worth.

Practical life skills included teaching people to cook, how to budget, to manage shopping, the use of public transport and other activities to enable independent living. In was not an easy process as very often tasks had to be broken down into numerous components and progress was often slow. Linked to the activities mentioned was the need for a programme of education to acquire numeracy and literacy skills. Through joint financing there was provision for the employment of further education tutors, and so they became part of the multi disciplinary team.

Social skills were another key area. To be able to function in the wider world it was and is essential to have an awareness of the importance of acceptable social skills and to be able to demonstrate this in social situations. Maybe inappropriate behaviour had been acquired in hospital, which whilst tolerated there, would not be accepted in the community. Opportunities for involvement with community activities were created to enable people to develop better social skills. In the wider sense the introduction of leisure and social opportunities was crucial for the future as a means of enhancing the quality of life. There was a concern that life in the community might lead to loneliness or boredom. Efforts were made to lessen the risk by encouraging relevant leisure and educational activities, mainly using existing community facilities. For some, employment was a realistic aim and so thought had to be given as to how to prepare people but also to develop links with employment agencies and in particular the Disablement Resettlement Officer. A number of people did secure employment and held jobs with ongoing support. Building confidence led to a willingness to tackle challenging situations, albeit within the individual's capability. Similarly having confidence enabled people to express their wishes and helped them to make decisions and to make informed choices. The more they achieved the greater was the confidence.

Throughout their stay at Aldingham Hall there were regular multi-disciplinary reviews of needs and progress, with thought given to future direction. Attention was focused on the person as an individual. As noted earlier three hundred people graduated from Aldingham Hall during its lifetime. Initially it was predicted that it would close after a year. Actually the service continued for five years. It was widely recognised both locally and nationally, as being a hugely successful enterprise. There was much interest shown from various bodies throughout the country, and indeed internationally, all wishing to learn from the expertise which had been built up. It received a National Social Care Award for excellence. Locally a research project had been established from the outset in order to objectively measure the success or indeed lack of success of the Aldingham Hall project. The results show that in terms of developmental progress for participants there had been significant gains compared with the control group in hospital.

The story does not end there, however, as this success created problems. Recipients of the service could not be returned to hospital at the end of their stay at Aldingham Hall. It would not have been fair on them, but also the objective of the project was to enable people to move from hospital. A wide network of alternative community services had to be developed. The Community Mental Handicap Team was established to support people, both ex hospital residents, but also many others who had never left the community. Facilities for respite care were provided for children and adults. This was useful support for carers but as well it moved the service from hospital to a community base. Links were established with housing agencies, local authority and not for profit organisations.

The Health Service was able to use some of its own surplus housing but demand was so great a wider network was required. In terms of normalisation it was in any case preferable to use ordinary community facilities. The employment services, education colleges, FE tutors were all important components of the overall service. A truly multi agency, multi-disciplinary effort.

Success was achieved through the drive, energy, enthusiasm, belief and commitment of the workers involved. Aldingham Hall helped to change the learning disability services in a fundamental way. Finally, recognition should be given to the users of the Aldingham Hall service. At the time it was a pioneering service and therefore there was uncertainty. Users of the service showed immense courage in taking that first major step from hospital to the unknown.

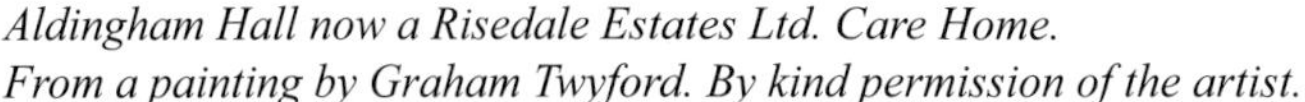
Aldingham Hall now a Risedale Estates Ltd. Care Home.
From a painting by Graham Twyford. By kind permission of the artist.

CHAPTER 8

CLOSURE

The whole philosophy towards people with learning disabilities changed following the publication of a Government White Paper in 1971 entitled "Better Services for Mentally Handicapped People". The White Paper stated that management of residents should be altered so that rather than providing hospital accommodation, training and support should be provided to enable them to live as independently as possible in the community.

There would be approximately 400 residents at Dovenby at this time and so it was envisaged by managers that the numbers would be slowly reduced as smaller units in the surrounding area were acquired and the less severely disabled residents gradually moved out into houses accommodating 6-8 people with support staff. This would involve co-operation between the Health Services and the Social Services Departments regarding staffing and finance. Unfortunately there appeared to be problems implementing these changes due to organisational divisions between the various authorities and the lack of adequate funding to enable the move from institutional to community care although emphasis on personal development and independence training continued for residents at Dovenby.

It was not until the Griffiths Report appeared in 1988 that major changes came about resulting in The Community Care White Paper, "Caring for People", published in 1989. This was incorporated into the NHS and Community Care Act of 1990 which covered the financial arrangements for residential care.

Directors of Social Services and Chief Executives of NHS Trusts were instructed to move forward with assessments of individual needs and adequate care arrangements. Care services would be mainly paid for by the local authority unless the client required health care in which case the NHS was responsible. Needless to say there were many differences of opinion as to who was accountable but by 1993 the North Cumbria Health Authority was required by the Northern Regional Health Authority to plan for the closure of long stay hospital accommodation at Dovenby Hall.

Closure is return to bad old days

Dovenby plan hits trouble

For Dovenby and its 260 residents and staff these were days of anxiety and insecurity. There were many letters to the press expressing concern about the impending closure particularly when the last 100 most severely disabled residents were to be discharged. Apart from opposition from staff and relatives, residents in the areas where the proposed community homes were to be sited were apprehensive about the effect a house for ex-Dovenby residents

£4m plan to house final 100 patients

would have on the value of their property and the general tone of the area. They accused the authorities of siting the homes in areas where land was cheaper. Public meetings were held where the authorities were charged with being too hasty to close Dovenby. It was felt in some quarters that a small village should be retained in the grounds of Dovenby for the most severely disabled.

In 1995 the organisations elected to set up the homes and provide care for the residents were:

- Walsingham Community Homes
- Community Integrated Care
- West House

One group of very elderly residents moved into a complete wing of Riverside Court, Maryport, together with the staff who had been looking after them at Dovenby. The wing was named the Ballantine Suite after the Ballantine Dykes family who had once lived at Dovenby Hall. Newspapers ran headlines that suggested that some elderly long- stay residents had died of broken hearts shortly after being moved from Dovenby to private nursing homes. These claims were vigorously denied by the Health Authority.

In all 19 houses were adapted for care in the community. In Egremont, Frizington, Hensingham, Moresby Parks, Carlisle, Wigton, Penrith, Aspatria, Workington, Maryport, Little Broughton, Flimby and Camerton. Each house has 6-8 residents with 24 hour care. The majority of the former nursing staff from Dovenby worked in the new community homes which at least provided some continuity for the residents.

If the departure from Dovenby was difficult for the residents, imagine how it must have been for the staff, some of whom had worked there for 30 years. Some families had seen two or three generations work at Dovenby. It was a massive provider of employment for a large area of West Cumbria. Many of the nursing staff who now worked with small groups in the community lost the opportunity to further their chosen career path.

Pension fears: No cause for panic — Union man tells Dovenby workers

Headlines courtesy Cumbrian Newspapers

Questions were asked about pension rights which had seemed so secure under the umbrella of the NHS. Union leaders fought hard for the rights of the staff who were losing or changing their jobs.

Counselling sessions by Mr Phil May and other members of the Health Service Psychology Department were offered to staff to help them over this traumatic period.

At the time of closure the buildings had become dilapidated as there was little funding for maintenance. This also had an effect on the staff who had always been very proud of the buildings and grounds.

In a report in the Times and Star on 26th March 1993, 18 long serving members of staff were presented with a framed pen and ink sketch of Dovenby Hall by Eric Urquhart, chairman of West Cumbria Health Care NHS Trust. Between them they had a total of 332 years service.

They included: Mrs Ann Ashcroft, linen room supervisor (16 years); George Blackman, night manager (9 years); Miss Lesley Cariss, behaviour therapy nurse (18 years); Mrs Alwyn Collister, Harston ward (19 years); Mrs Jean Crellin, sewing room supervisor (24 years); Mrs Ruby Ferguson, Howard Unit (27 years); Mrs Ina Garrett, Conway Ward (14 years); Mrs Sheila Graham, Howard Unit (18 years); Mrs Betty Hewitt, Eventide Club (22 years); Mrs Laura Hodgson, Howard Unit (30 years); Mrs Una Jackson, Punnett Ward (19 Years); Mrs Ellen Jansen, manager day services/The Elms (18 years); Mrs Irene Jefferson, domestic staff (13 years); Mrs Margaret Johnston, McHugh Ward (12 years); Mrs Nancy Nixon, finance department (20 years); Mrs Elizabeth Percival, day services (21 years); Mrs Mary Stephenson, Conway Ward (19 years).

The late Michael Baskett, Service Manager, on the left of the group is believed to have been responsible for the commissioning of the pen and ink sketch by A Donaldson..
Photo courtesy Times and Star. Sketch by A Donaldson

FINALE

"Dovenby goes out to the flicker of candles." (Times and Star headline)

Although all the residents had been moved out some time previously, Friday, January 31st 1997 marked the final closure of Dovenby Hall Hospital, 65 years after it opened its doors as a "Colony for Mental Defectives".

The following day, 1st February, a candlelit service of thanksgiving for all associated with Dovenby was held at 4pm, conducted by Rev. J. V. Hine, the hospital chaplain, assisted by the Rev. Tony Aubrey of the Free Evangelical Church, Little Broughton, and Malcolm Cowan, pastoral assistant at Bridekirk. It was attended by 200 people including former residents and their carers, doctors, social workers and representatives of the Health Authority. The service was organised by Dot Pickering, a former staff member who, together with Bill Stewart, a former resident, laid a wreath in tribute to all those who had died in the hospital, followed by two minutes silence.

As candles were lit for each of Dovenby's 65 years the Rev. Aubrey said,

"Today is the end of an era but the beginning of a new chapter."

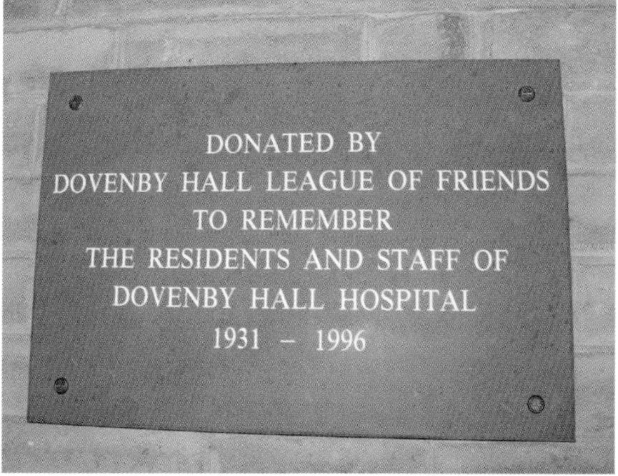

Memorial plaque in Bridekirk church. Photo Linda Davey

Margaret Hedley. Photo Dot Pickering

Above: (L) Marlene Smith (R) Molly Hyslop. Photo courtesy Times and Star

CHAPTER 9

THE M-SPORT STORY

Dovenby may have gone out to "the flicker of candles" but it was soon to roar back to life thanks to the vision of Malcolm Wilson O.B.E., a local man and former World Championship driver for the Ford Rally Team.

Malcolm Wilson and project manager Martyn Boak study plans for new M-Sport workshops.
Photo courtesy News and Star

Malcolm Wilson takes over Dovenby Hall Estate in 1997.
Photo courtesy News and Star

World Rally Manufacturer's Championship trophy 2006 & 2007.
Harold Burslem

Malcolm Wilson O.B.E. Managing Director M-Sport Ltd.
Photo courtesy M-Sport Ltd.

His company M-Sport Ltd. was originally set up in 1979 and after re- locating to its Dovenby headquarters in 1997 has successfully run Ford's World Rally Programme. M-Sport's award-winning engineering and design department also operates a thriving customer service for private teams.

Dovenby estate has been sympathetically and beautifully restored much to the delight of former residents and staff.

Aerial view of Dovenby circa 1970

Dovenby today. Photo courtesy M-Sport Ltd.

Some examples of the superb restoration of Dovenby

Linking the old with the new. Photographs by kind permission of Harold Burslem and M-Sport Ltd.

Copyright H. Burslem 1998

Copyright H. Burslem 2012

Corridor

Staircase

Oak panelled room

Dovenby entrance 1997. Photo Rodney Casson

Dovenby entrance today. Photo Peter Davey

WHITEHAVEN HOSPITAL RESEARCH GROUP

Whitehaven Hospital Research Group came into being in 2001 when some former nurses, doctors, pharmacists, voluntary workers and clerical staff got together to produce a history of Whitehaven Castle during the years it was used as a hospital 1926 – 1988. They recorded their memories of the time they worked there together with a history of nurse training and medical care in the Whitehaven area. The book which resulted from their investigations "Whitehaven Castle – The Hospital Years" was very well received after its launch in 2002 at The Beacon and went on to achieve a runner-up certificate in its category at the Lakeland Book of the Year Awards in 2003.

A commemorative plaque, recording the history of Whitehaven Castle, was commissioned by the group and erected at the entrance to the Castle Park in July 2009. It was unveiled by Nancy Rodgers a former nursing sister.

Since that time the group members have continued to meet to share information about health care today as well as retaining our interest in local history.

Lakeland Book of the Year Awards 2003. L to R:- Margaret Nelson, Linda Davey, Maureen Fisher and Nancy Rodgers

Unveiling of plaque 2009. L to R:- Rev. J Bannister, Violet Watson, Linda Davey, Nancy Rodgers, Margaret Nelson, Mildred Billington, Jilly Mitchell, Maureen Fisher, Annette Hill, Vera Moore, Mrs JoyceMcVeigh and Mr Michael McVeigh, Deputy Mayor of Copeland

Whitehaven Hospital Research Group

Standing L to R:- Nancy Rodgers, Vera Moore, Joan Davidson, Bernadette Crellin, Annette Hill, Linda Davey, Maureen Fisher, Violet Watson and Jilly Mitchell. Seated L to R:- Joan Warwick, Margaret Nelson, Edyth Stephenson and Mildred Billington

Acknowledgements

Our sincere thanks must go to:

- Lorraine Harper for 'planting' the idea of writing a book about Dovenby Hall.
- Alison Carswell and Service Users of Westlea Centre, Cockermouth for their encouragement.
- Pearl and Malcolm Wilson of M-Sport Ltd. for their interest and support.
- Nancy and Hugh Ballantine Dykes
- The members of Arlecdon History Group
- Cumbria Community Foundation for their advice regarding funding.
- Cumbrian Newspaper Group for their contribution towards publication costs and permission to use information and photographs.
- Harold Burslem for his invaluable help and photographs.
- Mervyn Dodd
- The Management and Staff of the Chase Hotel, Whitehaven, for use of accommodation by the research group.

Our very special thanks to everyone who contributed photographs and information.